LINUX MASTERY

A Comprehensive Guide for Beginners

and Beyond

Ryan Campbell

Table of Contents

INTRODUCTION TO LINUX 1

CHAPTER 1 4

Linux Installation Made Easy 4

CHAPTER 2 13

Understanding Linux Distributions 13

CHAPTER 3 25

Mastering the Linux Command Line 25

CHAPTER 4 37

Linux File System Explained 37

CHAPTER 5 48

Getting Hands-On 48

CHAPTER 6 61

Networking in Linux 61

CHAPTER 7 113

System Administration Essentials 113

CHAPTER 8..120

Advanced Linux Topics 120

CHAPTER 9..125

Linux in the Cloud 125

CONCLUSION 132

INTRODUCTION TO LINUX

Welcome to the captivating world of Linux, where digital adventures await, and the possibilities are boundless! If you've ever wondered what lies beneath the surface of this powerful operating system, then you've come to the right place. Get ready to embark on a thrilling journey, from absolute newcomer to a confident navigator of the Linux universe!

In this book, we'll take you by the hand and lead you through the exciting realms of Linux, step by exhilarating step. Whether you're a fresh-faced computer engineer, a tech enthusiast, or someone eager to embrace the open-source magic, we've got you covered. No prior Linux experience required – just a willingness to explore, learn, and discover!

Ever find yourself curious about that mysterious command line interface everyone's talking about? Fear not! We'll demystify the secrets of the Linux command line and unveil its hidden treasures, empowering you to unleash the full potential of this enigmatic OS.

But wait, there's more! We won't stop at the basics; we'll dive deep into the heart of Linux's file system, showing you how to navigate and manage your data like a pro. You'll learn to manipulate files with ease, organize your digital world, and feel like a digital mastermind in no time.

And let's not forget the thrill of practical exercises. Get your hands dirty with real-world applications and see your newfound knowledge come to life. It's time to break away from mundane theory and dive headfirst into the exciting world of Linux.

Are you curious about networking in Linux? Discover how to connect and secure your systems like a seasoned tech guru. Learn to protect your digital fortress from lurking threats and explore the vast possibilities of networking in the Linux universe.

But that's not all – our adventure doesn't end there! We'll also equip you with the essential skills of system administration. Take charge of your Linux environment, optimize performance, and become the hero of your digital kingdom.

Wait, there's even more to explore! For those who crave advanced knowledge and aspire to rise to the top, we've got a special treat for you. Elevate your expertise with in-depth discussions on advanced Linux topics, catering to your insatiable appetite for knowledge.

And let's not forget the horizon of technology – Linux in the cloud! Peek into the future of computing as Linux embraces the cloud era. This is your ticket to staying ahead of the game and surfing the waves of tomorrow's digital landscape.

So, fellow tech explorer, are you ready to take the plunge? If you seek adventure, knowledge, and the power to conquer the digital realm, then join us as we journey from novice to confident Linux navigator. It's time to embrace the exciting challenges that await you on this thrilling ride!

Get your gear ready, and let's dive into the world of Linux – where the only limit is your imagination! Are you ready? Let's go!

CHAPTER 1

Linux Installation Made Easy

Setting Up Your System Hassle-Free

Embrace the Freedom of Linux

Welcome to the world of Linux, a realm of open-source wonders, boundless possibilities, and creative freedom! If you're new to Linux, you're about to embark on an exciting journey that will revolutionize the way you interact with your computer. Unlike proprietary operating systems, Linux offers you the power to customize, optimize, and mold your digital experience to suit your unique needs.

This chapter is your gateway to the Linux adventure, where we will guide you through the process of installing Linux on your system seamlessly. Whether you're a tech enthusiast, a curious explorer, or a professional looking to expand your skills, we've got you covered. Let's dive into the world of Linux installation, where we'll show you how to set up your system hassle-free, ensuring a smooth ride from start to finish.

1.1 Why Choose Linux?

Before we delve into the installation process, let's briefly explore why Linux has gained immense popularity and why it might be the perfect fit for you.

0   1.1.1 Open-Source Freedom

One of the key attractions of Linux is its open-source nature. Unlike closed-source operating systems, Linux is developed and maintained by a global community of dedicated individuals and organizations. This collaborative effort results in a system that is continuously improving, secure, and customizable to meet various needs.

1   1.1.2 Diverse Distributions

Linux comes in various distributions, each tailored to specific use cases and preferences. From beginner-friendly distributions like Ubuntu and Linux Mint to powerful ones like Fedora and Arch Linux, you have a plethora of choices to find the one that suits you best.

2   1.1.3 Stability and Reliability

Linux is renowned for its stability and reliability. It can run for extended periods without requiring a reboot and is less prone to crashes and viruses. For professionals seeking a robust environment for critical tasks or developers looking for a stable platform, Linux is a natural choice.

3   1.1.4 Security and Privacy

With its open-source nature, Linux undergoes rigorous security audits by the community, making it inherently more secure. Moreover, Linux provides robust privacy options, allowing you to take control of your data and digital footprint.

4   1.1.5 Cost-Effective

Unlike some proprietary operating systems that come with hefty price tags, Linux is free to use. It empowers you to access powerful tools and capabilities without breaking the bank.

5   1.1.6 Vast Software Repositories

Linux offers extensive software repositories filled with thousands of free and open-source applications. Whatever your needs, you're likely to find a suitable software tool to get the job done.

6   1.1.7 Versatility and Scalability

Whether you're using Linux on your personal computer, in a server environment, or on embedded devices, it adapts effortlessly. Its versatility and scalability make it an ideal choice for a wide range of applications.

1.2 Preparing for Linux Installation

Before we dive into the installation process, it's essential to make some preparations to ensure a smooth journey.

7   1.2.1 Backup Your Data

Installing an operating system involves making changes to your computer's storage. As a precautionary measure, back up all your important data to an external drive or cloud storage to prevent any accidental loss during the installation process.

8 1.2.2 Choose the Right Linux Distribution

As mentioned earlier, Linux comes in various distributions, each with its own unique features and user interface. Take some time to research different distributions and select the one that aligns with your needs and preferences. If you're new to Linux, beginner-friendly distributions like Ubuntu or Linux Mint are excellent choices.

9 1.2.3 Check System Requirements

Different Linux distributions have varying system requirements. Ensure that your computer meets the minimum hardware specifications for the distribution you've chosen.

10 1.2.4 Create a Bootable USB Drive or DVD

Once you've selected a Linux distribution, create a bootable USB drive or burn it onto a DVD. This will be your installation media, allowing you to install Linux on your system.

11 1.2.5 Free Up Disk Space

Before installation, make sure you have sufficient free disk space on your computer. Linux requires some space for installation and operation. If your disk is nearly full, consider freeing up space by removing unnecessary files or applications.

12 1.2.6 Familiarize Yourself with BIOS/UEFI Settings

Depending on your computer's hardware, you may need to make some changes to the BIOS or UEFI settings to ensure a successful installation. Review the documentation for your computer or motherboard to understand the necessary adjustments.

1.3 Installing Linux: Step-by-Step Guide

Step 1: Boot from Installation Media

Insert the bootable USB drive or DVD into your computer's appropriate slot. Restart your computer and boot from the installation media. Typically, you can access the boot menu by pressing a specific key (e.g., F12, F2, or Delete) during startup. Choose the option that corresponds to the installation media.

Once the boot process is complete, you'll be presented with the Linux distribution's welcome screen.

Step 2: Check System Compatibility

Next, the installer will check your computer's hardware compatibility. If any issues are detected, the installer will alert you, and you may need to address them before proceeding.

Step 3: Choose Installation Type

At this stage, you'll be asked to select the installation type. If you're new to Linux or wish to replace your current operating system, choose the "Erase disk and install Linux" option. This will remove your existing operating system and all data on the disk, so make sure you've backed up your data as mentioned earlier. If you prefer a dual-boot setup, choose the appropriate option to install Linux alongside your existing operating system.

Step 4: Set Time Zone and Keyboard Layout

Select your time zone and keyboard layout. These settings ensure that your system's time is accurate and that you can type comfortably.

Step 5: Create User Account

Now it's time to create your user account. Choose a username and password, and optionally, the computer's name. This account will have administrator privileges, allowing you to make system changes and install software.

Step 6: Installation Progress

After confirming your settings, the installation process will begin. Sit back, relax, and let the installer work its magic.

Step 7: Installation Complete

Remove the installation media, and your computer will boot into your brand-new Linux operating system!

1.4 Post-Installation Steps

Congratulations! You've successfully installed Linux on your system. Now, there are a few post-installation steps to ensure you have a smooth and enjoyable Linux experience.

13 1.4.1 Update Your System

After the installation, it's essential to update your Linux system to ensure you have the latest software and security patches. Open the terminal, and depending on your Linux distribution, use the appropriate package manager command to update the system. For example, on Debian-based systems like Ubuntu, use the following command:

sqlCopy code

sudo apt update sudo apt upgrade

On RPM-based systems like Fedora, use:

sqlCopy code

sudo dnf update

This will fetch the latest updates from the software repositories and apply them to your system.

14 1.4.2 Install Essential Software

While most Linux distributions come with a variety of pre-installed software, you may want to install additional applications that suit your needs. Linux offers a vast array of software available through its package manager. For example, you can install a web browser, productivity tools, media players, and more. Explore the software repositories and discover the applications that align with your preferences.

15 1.4.3 Customization and Desktop Environments

One of the beauties of Linux is its customizability. You can personalize your desktop environment to match your style and workflow. Whether you prefer a sleek, minimalist desktop or a feature-rich one, Linux has you covered. Experiment with different themes, icons, and desktop layouts to create your ideal digital workspace.

16 1.4.4 Explore the Linux Ecosystem

Now that you have Linux up and running, it's time to explore the vast Linux ecosystem. Join online forums, communities, and social media groups to connect with other Linux enthusiasts. Seek help, share knowledge, and be part of the vibrant open-source community. Linux users are known for their willingness to help newcomers, so don't hesitate to ask questions or share your experiences.

17 1.4.5 Troubleshooting and Support

As you navigate your Linux journey, you might encounter some challenges or issues. Linux has robust documentation and a wealth of online resources to help you troubleshoot and find solutions to common problems. Embrace the challenge and enjoy the satisfaction of conquering obstacles on your path to Linux mastery.

Conclusion: Embrace Your Linux Adventure

You've conquered the installation process and set up your system hassle-free. From here on, your Linux adventure is limited only by your curiosity and creativity.

Remember that Linux is a powerful tool that can transform your digital experience. As you dive deeper into the Linux ecosystem, you'll discover new possibilities and unlock the potential of your computer. Don't be afraid to experiment, learn, and grow with Linux – it's a journey that rewards curiosity and passion.

In the upcoming chapters, we'll delve deeper into the Linux operating system, exploring its core concepts, command-line interface, file system, networking, and system administration. With each chapter, you'll gain new skills and insights, empowering you to become a confident Linux user and explorer.

So, buckle up and get ready for an exhilarating ride through the exciting realms of Linux. Whether you're a tech enthusiast, a developer, a professional, or just a curious explorer, Linux has something incredible in store for you. Let's dive in together and embrace the freedom, power, and limitless potential of Linux! Are you ready? Let's go!

CHAPTER 2

UNDERSTANDING LINUX DISTRIBUTIONS

Finding Your Perfect Fit

The Diverse World of Linux Distributions

Welcome to the exciting realm of Linux distributions! As you journey deeper into the Linux universe, you'll quickly discover that Linux comes in various flavors, each tailored to specific use cases, preferences, and skill levels. In this chapter, we'll dive into the diverse world of Linux distributions, helping you find the perfect fit that aligns with your needs and aspirations.

Whether you're a newcomer seeking a beginner-friendly experience, a power user craving customization and control, a developer in pursuit of cutting-edge tools, or a system administrator managing large-scale deployments, there's a Linux distribution out there waiting to be your digital companion.

Let's embark on this voyage of exploration, as we unveil the unique features, strengths, and communities behind some of the most popular Linux distributions. By the end of this chapter, you'll be well-equipped to make an informed decision and set sail on your Linux journey with the distribution that resonates with you.

2.1 What is a Linux Distribution?

Before we delve into the individual distributions, let's grasp the concept of a Linux distribution. In the world of Linux, the term "distribution" refers to a complete operating system package that includes the Linux kernel, essential system utilities, libraries, and a package manager to manage software installations and updates.

A Linux distribution is essentially a cohesive bundle of software components, bundled together with a specific set of configurations and a unique identity. Each distribution may have its own default desktop environment, package manager, system administration tools, and software repositories.

2.2 Popular Linux Distributions

Let's explore some of the most popular Linux distributions that have gained a strong following over the years.

18 2.2.1 Ubuntu

Overview: Ubuntu is one of the most well-known and widely used Linux distributions, renowned for its user-friendly approach and focus on ease of use. It is based on the Debian architecture and follows a regular six-month release cycle. Ubuntu offers long-term support (LTS) versions for stable and reliable performance, making it suitable for both beginners and advanced users.

Target Audience: Ubuntu is ideal for newcomers to Linux who value a polished and straightforward desktop experience. It caters to a broad user base, including home users, students, developers, and small businesses.

Default Desktop Environment: Ubuntu uses the GNOME desktop environment by default, providing a clean and intuitive interface.

Package Manager: Ubuntu employs the Advanced Package Tool (APT) for managing software installations and updates.

19 2.2.2 Fedora

Overview: Fedora is a cutting-edge Linux distribution sponsored by Red Hat. It emphasizes the integration of the latest software packages and technologies, making it a favorite among developers and technology enthusiasts. Fedora follows a rapid release cycle and prides itself on being at the forefront of open-source innovation.

Target Audience: Fedora is ideal for tech-savvy users, developers, and enthusiasts who crave the latest features and advancements in the Linux ecosystem.

Default Desktop Environment: Fedora's default desktop environment is GNOME, providing a sleek and modern user experience.

Package Manager: Fedora uses the DNF (Dandified Yum) package manager, which is an evolution of the traditional Yum package manager.

20 2.2.3 Linux Mint

Overview: Linux Mint is a user-friendly distribution based on Ubuntu, with a focus on providing an elegant and intuitive desktop experience. It strives to be a practical and familiar platform for both newcomers and experienced users alike.

Target Audience: Linux Mint is perfect for users who seek a familiar and comfortable desktop environment similar to traditional operating systems.

Default Desktop Environment: Linux Mint offers multiple editions with different desktop environments, with the Cinnamon desktop being the most popular and user-friendly choice.

Package Manager: Like Ubuntu, Linux Mint utilizes the APT package manager for software management.

21 2.2.4 Debian

Overview: Debian is one of the oldest and most respected Linux distributions, known for its stability and commitment to free and open-source principles. It serves as the foundation for many other distributions, including Ubuntu.

Target Audience: Debian is suitable for users who prioritize stability and reliability over the latest features. It is often chosen for servers, large deployments, and systems that require long-term support.

Default Desktop Environment: Debian offers multiple desktop environment options, including GNOME, KDE Plasma, Xfce, and others.

Package Manager: Debian employs APT as its package manager, making it easy to manage software installations and updates.

22 2.2.5 Arch Linux

Overview: Arch Linux is a minimalist and highly customizable distribution designed for experienced users who enjoy building their Linux systems from the ground up. It follows a rolling release model, meaning users continuously receive the latest updates and features.

Target Audience: Arch Linux appeals to seasoned Linux users, developers, and enthusiasts who value customization and full control over their system.

Default Desktop Environment: Arch Linux does not come with a default desktop environment, allowing users to choose their preferred environment during installation.

Package Manager: Arch Linux uses the Pacman package manager, known for its speed and efficiency in managing software packages.

23 2.2.6 CentOS

Overview: CentOS (Community Enterprise Operating System) is a Linux distribution based on the source code of Red Hat Enterprise Linux (RHEL). It is designed to provide a free, stable, and compatible alternative to RHEL, making it a popular choice for servers and enterprise deployments.

Target Audience: CentOS is tailored for users seeking a stable and enterprise-ready Linux distribution without the associated licensing costs.

Default Desktop Environment: CentOS is primarily used as a server operating system and does not come with a default desktop environment. However, users can install one if needed.

Package Manager: CentOS uses YUM (Yellowdog Updater Modified) as its package manager, which is compatible with RHEL's package management system.

2.3 Specialized Distributions

In addition to the popular distributions mentioned above, the Linux ecosystem offers a plethora of specialized distributions catering to niche use cases. Let's explore a few noteworthy examples:

24 2.3.1 Kali Linux

Overview: Kali Linux is a specialized distribution designed for penetration testing and ethical hacking. It comes preloaded with a vast collection of tools for security professionals and enthusiasts.

Target Audience: Kali Linux is targeted at security professionals, network administrators, and ethical hackers who require a powerful platform for testing network and system vulnerabilities.

Default Desktop Environment: Kali Linux uses the GNOME desktop environment, providing a familiar and user-friendly interface.

Package Manager: Kali Linux utilizes APT as its package manager for software management.

25 2.3.2 Raspbian

Overview: Raspbian is a Linux distribution tailored for the Raspberry Pi single-board computers. It is optimized for performance on these small devices and comes with pre-installed software for various projects and tasks.

Target Audience: Raspbian is aimed at hobbyists, educators, and developers who want to explore the capabilities of the Raspberry Pi.

Default Desktop Environment: Raspbian's default desktop environment is LXDE, a lightweight and resource-friendly environment suitable for the Raspberry Pi's limited hardware.

Package Manager: Raspbian uses APT as its package manager, making it easy to install software on the Raspberry Pi.

2.4 Choosing Your Ideal Distribution

With the multitude of Linux distributions available, you may wonder how to select the one that best suits your needs and preferences. The key to finding your ideal Linux distribution lies in understanding your goals, preferences, and technical expertise. Let's walk through a series of considerations to help you make an informed decision:

26 2.4.1 Purpose and Use Case

Begin by defining the primary purpose of your Linux installation. Are you looking for a desktop operating system for general use, web browsing, and office productivity? In this case, user-friendly distributions like Ubuntu, Linux Mint, or Fedora may be the best options.

On the other hand, if you are a developer seeking cutting-edge tools and a rolling release model, Arch Linux might be the way to go. For server environments, CentOS or Debian could be the preferred choices due to their stability and long-term support.

If your focus is on network security and penetration testing, Kali Linux is the go-to distribution. For Raspberry Pi projects, Raspbian is tailored to the unique hardware requirements of the tiny computer.

27 2.4.2 Technical Experience

Your level of technical expertise is an essential factor in choosing a Linux distribution. If you're a newcomer to Linux or prefer a smooth, out-of-the-box experience, user-friendly distributions like Ubuntu, Linux Mint, or Fedora are recommended.

For those who enjoy tinkering with the system and configuring it to their liking, Arch Linux's DIY approach might be an exciting challenge. Experienced Linux users who prioritize stability and control may find Debian or CentOS to be a perfect fit.

28 2.4.3 Hardware Compatibility

Consider the hardware on which you plan to install Linux. Some distributions have specific hardware requirements, and certain drivers may not be readily available for all distributions. If you're installing Linux on older hardware, distributions known for their lightweight and efficient performance, such as Xubuntu or Lubuntu, may be more suitable.

For compatibility with specific hardware components, check the respective distribution's documentation and community forums for user experiences and recommendations.

29 2.4.4 Desktop Environment Preferences

The desktop environment greatly influences the user experience. If you have a preference for a particular desktop environment, consider distributions that come with it as the default option. Remember that you can install and switch between different desktop environments on most distributions after installation.

30 2.4.5 Community and Support

The strength of a distribution's community and support resources can greatly impact your Linux journey. Larger and more active communities tend to provide better documentation, tutorials, and forums for troubleshooting.

Ubuntu, being one of the most popular distributions, has a massive and active community. Similarly, Fedora, Debian, and Arch Linux have robust communities that can offer valuable guidance and support.

31 2.4.6 Package Management

Package management systems handle software installations, updates, and removals on Linux. Some distributions use APT, while others use DNF, YUM, or Pacman. Familiarize yourself with the package manager of your chosen distribution to ensure you are comfortable using it.

32 2.4.7 Long-Term Support (LTS)

If you require a stable and long-term supported system, consider distributions that offer LTS releases. Ubuntu, for instance, provides LTS versions with extended support for several years, making it suitable for users who prefer not to upgrade frequently.

33 2.4.8 Customizability

If customization is a priority for you, distributions like Arch Linux and Fedora allow you to build your system from the ground up and tailor it to your exact needs. Look for distributions that provide flexibility in choosing desktop environments, software packages, and system configurations.

34 2.4.9 Virtual Machine Testing

If you are uncertain about which distribution to choose, consider using a virtual machine to test various distributions without affecting your primary operating system. Virtualization software like VirtualBox or VMware allows you to create virtual machines and install different Linux distributions for evaluation.

35 2.4.10 Dual-Boot Considerations

If you intend to dual-boot Linux alongside another operating system, ensure that the distribution you choose supports dual-boot installations. Some distributions have user-friendly installers that make dual-boot setups straightforward.

Conclusion: Finding Your Linux Adventure

As you explore the world of Linux distributions, you'll discover a vibrant ecosystem of options tailored to every taste and requirement. Each distribution brings its unique strengths, features, and communities to the table, offering a diverse range of experiences to users worldwide.

Remember that the best Linux distribution for you is the one that aligns with your goals, technical expertise, and preferences. Whether you're seeking a beginner-friendly desktop environment, a powerful developer's toolkit, a stable server platform, or a specialized security toolkit, there's a Linux distribution that will match your aspirations.

Choose with confidence, knowing that you are embarking on a Linux adventure filled with freedom, innovation, and the power to shape your digital world. The journey doesn't end here; it's only just begun. In the subsequent chapters, we'll delve deeper into the core concepts of Linux, exploring the command-line interface, the file system, system administration, and more.

So, what are you waiting for? Take the plunge, choose your Linux distribution, and unlock the boundless potential that Linux offers. Your adventure awaits – and it starts with your perfect fit! Happy Linux exploring!

CHAPTER 3

MASTERING THE LINUX COMMAND LINE

Unleashing the Full Power

The Command Line - A Gateway to Power

Welcome to the heart of Linux, where the real magic happens - the command-line interface (CLI). While graphical user interfaces (GUIs) offer a user-friendly experience, the command line opens a world of limitless possibilities, allowing you to interact with Linux at its core. In this chapter, we'll take you on a journey through the Linux command line, empowering you with the knowledge and skills to harness its full potential.

The command line might seem daunting at first, but fear not! With every command, you'll gain more confidence, and soon you'll be wielding the power of Linux like a seasoned pro. By mastering the command line, you'll find efficiency, speed, and the ability to perform complex tasks with ease - essential skills for any Linux user, be it a developer, sysadmin, or a curious explorer.

Let's dive into the world of the Linux command line and unlock its full power together!

3.1 Getting to Know the Command Line

36 3.1.1 The Terminal Emulator

The command-line interface is accessed through a terminal emulator, a text-based window that allows you to interact with the Linux system using commands. Common terminal emulators include GNOME Terminal, Konsole, and Xfce Terminal, among others. When you open a terminal, you'll be greeted with a command prompt, where you can enter commands and execute them.

37 3.1.2 Basic Command Structure

Linux commands follow a straightforward structure: **command [options] [arguments]**. The command is the action you want to perform, options modify the behavior of the command, and arguments are the items on which the command operates. Some commands can be as simple as **ls** to list files in a directory, while others may require more complex syntax.

38 3.1.3 Command Autocompletion

The command-line interface is designed for efficiency, and one powerful feature is tab completion. When typing a command or file path, pressing the **Tab** key will automatically complete the command or suggest possible options, saving you time and reducing typing errors.

39 3.1.4 Command History

The terminal keeps track of your command history, allowing you to navigate through previous commands using the arrow keys. This feature makes it easy to repeat or modify previous commands without re-typing them.

3.2 Essential Linux Commands

Let's explore some essential Linux commands that are fundamental to mastering the command line.

40 3.2.1 ls - Listing Files and Directories

The **ls** command is used to list files and directories in the current directory. By default, it displays a simple list of filenames. To see additional information, you can use options such as **-l** for a long format or **-a** to show hidden files.

Example:

bashCopy code

ls ls -l ls -a

41 3.2.2 cd - Changing the Current Directory

Use **cd** followed by the directory path to move to the desired location.

Example:

bashCopy code

cd /home/user/documents

42 3.2.3 pwd - Present Working Directory

The **pwd** command displays the absolute path of the current working directory. It can be handy when you need to confirm your current location in the file system.

Example:

bashCopy code

pwd

43 3.2.4 mkdir - Creating Directories

Example:

arduinoCopy code

mkdir new_folder

44 3.2.5 touch - Creating Files

The **touch** command creates new, empty files. If the file already exists, it updates the file's modification time. Use **touch** followed by the filename to create a new file.

Example:

bashCopy code

touch new_file.txt

45 3.2.6 cp - Copying Files and Directories

Use **cp** followed by the source file or directory and the destination.

Example:

bashCopy code

cp file.txt /home/user/documents/

46 3.2.7 mv - Moving and Renaming Files and Directories

This is used to rename files or directories. Use **mv** followed by the source and destination.

Example:

bashCopy code

mv file.txt /home/user/documents/ mv file.txt new_file.txt

47 3.2.8 rm - Removing Files and Directories

To remove a file, use **rm** followed by the filename.

Example:

bashCopy code

rm file.txt rm -r directory/

48 3.2.9 grep - Searching for Text

It searches for a specific pattern or text in files and outputs the matching lines. Use **grep** followed by the search term and the filename(s) to search.

Example:

perlCopy code

grep "keyword" file.txt

49 3.2.10 man - Accessing the Manual

The **man** command provides access to the Linux manual pages, which contain detailed information and usage examples for various commands. Simply use **man** followed by the command you want to learn more about.

Example:

bashCopy code

man ls

3.3 Redirection and Piping

One of the command line's strengths lies in its ability to manipulate data using redirection and piping.

50 3.3.1 Redirection (> and >>)

Redirection allows you to control where the output of a command is sent. The **>** symbol is used to redirect the output of a command to a file, overwriting its contents if the file already exists. On the other hand, the **>>** symbol appends the output to the end of the file.

Example of **>**:

bashCopy code

ls > file_list.txt

This command will list the contents of the current directory and save the output to a file called **file_list.txt**.

Example of **>>**:

bashCopy code

ls >> file_list.txt

This command will list the contents of the current directory and append the output to the end of the file **file_list.txt**.

Example:

bashCopy code

ls | grep "file"

In this example, the **ls** command lists the files in the current directory, and the output is then passed to the **grep** command to search for lines containing the word "file." This way, you can perform more complex operations by combining multiple commands together.

3.4 Advanced Command Line Techniques

51 3.4.1 Command Substitution ($())

Command substitution allows you to use the output of a command as part of another command. The syntax for command substitution is **$(command)**. It is particularly useful when you need to store the output of a command in a variable or use it as an argument for another command.

Example:

bashCopy code

current_date=$(date) echo "Today is $current_date"

In this example, the **$(date)** command retrieves the current date and time, which is then stored in the **current_date** variable. The **echo** command then displays the value of the **current_date** variable along with a custom message.

52 3.4.2 Wildcards (*, ?, [ ])

Wildcards are special characters used for pattern matching in the command line. They allow you to select multiple files or directories based on a pattern. The most commonly used wildcards are:

- *****: Matches any sequence of characters.

- **?**: Matches any single character.

- **[ ]**: Matches any character within the brackets.

Example:

bashCopy code

ls *.txt

This command lists all files in the current directory with the **.txt** extension.

53 3.4.3 Command Line Options and Arguments

Many Linux commands come with various options and arguments that modify their behavior. Options are typically specified using a single letter preceded by a hyphen, such as **-l** or **-a**. Multiple options can be combined, such as **-la**.

Example:

bashCopy code

ls -la

This command lists all files in the current directory, including hidden files, and displays detailed information in a long format.

54 3.4.4 sudo - Superuser Do

The **sudo** command is used to execute a command with superuser (root) privileges. Some operations, such as system administration tasks or installing software system-wide, require elevated privileges. Be cautious when using **sudo**, as it grants you access to critical system files and operations.

Example:

sqlCopy code

sudo apt update

This command updates the system's package list using the package manager with superuser privileges.

3.5 Command Line Efficiency Tips

As you continue to master the Linux command line, consider adopting these efficiency tips:

- **Use tab completion:** Take advantage of tab completion to quickly complete filenames, directories, and command names. It saves time and minimizes typing errors.

- **Learn keyboard shortcuts:** Mastering keyboard shortcuts can greatly enhance your command line experience. For example, **Ctrl + C** interrupts the current process, and **Ctrl + D** indicates the end of input.

- **Use history and search:** Utilize the command history to access previous commands quickly. Press the **up** and **down** arrow keys to navigate through history.

Additionally, use **Ctrl + R** to search for commands based on keywords.

- **Write shell scripts:** As you gain confidence with the command line, consider writing shell scripts to automate repetitive tasks. Shell scripting allows you to bundle a series of commands into a single executable file.

- **Practice and experiment:** The command line is a powerful tool with a wealth of possibilities.

Conclusion: The Command Line Adventure Continues

Congratulations! You've taken your first steps toward mastering the Linux command line and unlocking its full potential. Embrace the command line as a gateway to power, efficiency, and endless possibilities.

In this chapter, we explored essential Linux commands, learned about redirection and piping, and delved into advanced techniques like command substitution and wildcards. Armed with this knowledge, you can now navigate the command line landscape with confidence and precision.

In the next chapter, we'll dive even deeper into the Linux command line, exploring file system navigation, file manipulation, text processing, and more.

So, buckle up and get ready for an exciting continuation of your command line adventure. The world of Linux awaits, and the command line is your key to unleash its full power! Happy exploring!

CHAPTER 4

LINUX FILE SYSTEM EXPLAINED

Navigating and Managing Your Data

The Backbone of Linux

Behind every Linux system lies a sophisticated file system that organizes and manages data with precision and efficiency. Understanding the Linux file system is essential for any user, as it lays the foundation for effective data management and organization. In this chapter, we'll demystify the Linux file system, guiding you through its hierarchical structure, directory navigation, file permissions, and various essential concepts.

Whether you're a curious user, a developer, or a system administrator, mastering the Linux file system will empower you to manage your data with ease and optimize your digital workflow. Let's embark on this journey of exploration and uncover the secrets of the Linux file system together.

4.1 The Hierarchical File System

Linux follows a hierarchical file system structure, resembling an inverted tree. At the top of the tree is the root directory represented by a forward slash */*. Every file and directory in Linux resides within this hierarchical structure. Each directory can contain files and subdirectories, creating a nested arrangement.

55 4.1.1 Root Directory and Home Directory

The root directory, denoted as **/**, is the highest level of the file system and serves as the parent of all other directories. It is the starting point for navigating the file system.

Each user on a Linux system has a home directory, typically located at **/home/username**. The home directory is a user's personal space, where they can store files, create subdirectories, and access their own configurations.

56 4.1.2 Absolute and Relative Paths

Paths in Linux can be expressed as absolute or relative. An absolute path specifies the exact location of a file or directory from the root directory, starting with **/**. For example, **/home/user/documents/file.txt** is an absolute path.

On the other hand, a relative path refers to a location relative to the current working directory. For example, if the current working directory is **/home/user/documents**, the relative path to **file.txt** in the same directory is simply **file.txt**.

4.2 Navigating the File System

Understanding how to navigate the file system is fundamental to working efficiently on the Linux command line.

57 4.2.1 pwd - Present Working Directory

As mentioned in the previous chapter, the **pwd** command displays the absolute path of the current working directory.

Example:

bashCopy code

pwd

58 4.2.2 cd - Changing Directories

You can move to a specific directory using either an absolute or relative path.

Example:

bashCopy code

cd /home/user/documents cd ../pictures

The first command moves to the **documents** directory, while the second command moves up one level using **..** and then enters the **pictures** directory.

59 4.2.3 ls - Listing Files and Directories

The **ls** command, covered in the previous chapter, lists the contents of the current directory.

Example:

bashCopy code

ls

60 4.2.4 ls with Options

Adding options to the **ls** command enhances the output. For example, **ls -l** provides a detailed, long-format listing, and **ls -a** shows hidden files and directories.

Example:

bashCopy code

ls -l ls -a

61 4.2.5 ls with Paths

You can use the **ls** command with specific paths to list the contents of a particular directory without changing the current working directory.

Example:

bashCopy code

ls /home/user/documents ls ../pictures

The first command lists the contents of the **documents** directory, while the second command lists the contents of the **pictures** directory in the parent directory.

62 4.2.6 cd with No Arguments

Using **cd** without any arguments takes you to your home directory.

Example:

bashCopy code

cd

This command takes you to your home directory, regardless of the current working directory.

4.3 File and Directory Management

Managing files and directories is a crucial aspect of working with the Linux file system. Understanding how to create, copy, move, and remove files and directories is essential for effective data organization.

63 4.3.1 mkdir - Creating Directories

The **mkdir** command, also covered in the previous chapter, is used to create new directories.

Example:

arduinoCopy code

mkdir new_directory

This command creates a new directory named **new_directory** in the current working directory.

64 4.3.2 touch - Creating Files

The **touch** command, also covered earlier, creates new, empty files.

Example:

bashCopy code

touch new_file.txt

65 4.3.3 cp - Copying Files and Directories

The **cp** command, covered earlier, is used to copy files and directories from one location to another.

Example:

bashCopy code

cp file.txt /home/user/documents/

This command copies the file **file.txt** to the **documents** directory in the user's home directory.

66 4.3.4 mv - Moving and Renaming Files and Directories

The **mv** command, also covered earlier, moves files and directories from one location to another.

Example:

bashCopy code

mv file.txt /home/user/documents/ mv file.txt new_file.txt

The first command moves **file.txt** to the **documents** directory, and the second command renames **file.txt** to **new_file.txt** in the current directory.

67 4.3.5 rm - Removing Files and Directories

The **rm** command, covered earlier, is used to remove files and directories.

Example:

bashCopy code

rm file.txt rm -r directory/

The first command removes the file **file.txt**, and the second command removes the directory **directory** and its contents using the **-r** option, which stands for recursive.

68 4.3.6 rmdir - Removing Empty Directories

It is similar to **rm**, but it can only delete directories that have no files or subdirectories inside.

Example:

arduinoCopy code

rmdir empty_directory

This command removes the empty directory named **empty_directory**.

69 4.3.7 File Permissions

In the Linux file system, each file and directory has permissions that determine who can read, write, and execute them. Understanding file permissions is vital for security and managing access to sensitive data.

File permissions are represented by a three-character string, such as **rwx**. Each character indicates a specific permission: **r** for read, **w** for write, and **x** for execute. These permissions are organized into three groups: owner, group, and others.

To view the permissions of files and directories, you can use the **ls -l** command, which displays the permissions in the first column of the output.

Example:

bashCopy code

ls -l

This command lists the files and directories in the current directory, along with their permissions.

70 4.3.8 Changing File Permissions - chmod

You can modify permissions using either the octal notation or the symbolic notation.

71 Octal Notation

In octal notation, each permission is represented by a three-digit number. The digit 7 indicates full permission (read, write, and execute), 6 indicates read and write permission, 5 indicates read and execute permission, 4 indicates read-only permission, 3 indicates write and execute permission, 2 indicates write-only permission, and 1 indicates execute-only permission.

Example:

bashCopy code

chmod 755 file.txt

This command grants the owner read, write, and execute permission, and the group and others read and execute permission on **file.txt**.

72 Symbolic Notation

In symbolic notation, you can use symbols to add (**+**), remove (**-**), or set (**=**) permissions.

Example:

bashCopy code

chmod u+rwx file.txt chmod go-w file.txt

The first command adds read, write, and execute permission to the user (owner) of **file.txt**. The second command removes write permission from the group and others, leaving only read and execute permissions.

4.4 File System Navigation Tips

Navigating the Linux file system efficiently can save you time and make your work more enjoyable. Consider adopting these tips to enhance your file system navigation skills:

- **Use Tab Completion:** As mentioned in previous chapters, tab completion is a powerful tool for quickly completing filenames and directory names. Press the **Tab** key while typing to auto-complete names.

- **Create Meaningful Directory Structure:** Organize your directories logically and give them descriptive names. A well-structured file system makes it easier to find and manage your data.

- **Avoid Using Spaces in Filenames:** Although Linux allows spaces in filenames, using underscores or dashes instead is recommended. Spaces can sometimes lead to confusion when using commands on files with complex names.

- **Use cd - to Toggle Between Directories:** The **cd -** command allows you to toggle between the current and previous directories. It can be handy when you need to switch back and forth between two directories quickly.

- **Make Use of Symlinks:** Symlinks (symbolic links) are special files that point to another file or directory. They allow you to create shortcuts to frequently accessed files or navigate between directories more efficiently.

Conclusion: Mastery of the Linux File System

Congratulations! You have now demystified the Linux file system, learned how to navigate its hierarchical structure, and gained the knowledge to manage files and directories effectively.

The Linux file system forms the backbone of the operating system, providing the framework for organizing data and enabling users to interact with their digital world. By understanding the command line, file permissions, and various file management techniques, you are equipped to harness the power of Linux to its fullest.

As you continue your journey with Linux, remember that the file system is a canvas waiting for your creativity and organization. Embrace the challenge of building a well-structured file system, and let it become the foundation for your productivity and efficiency.

In the next chapter, we'll delve into the fascinating world of text processing on the Linux command line, where you'll learn how to manipulate and analyze textual data with ease. So, brace yourself for a text-tastic adventure ahead!

Happy navigating and managing your data with Linux!

CHAPTER 5

GETTING HANDS-ON

Practical Exercises for Real-World Application

Learning by Doing

Congratulations on your journey through the Linux command line, file system, and beyond! In this chapter, we'll take your learning experience to the next level by engaging in practical exercises that will reinforce your understanding of Linux concepts and empower you to apply your newfound knowledge in real-world scenarios.

Learning by doing is a powerful approach, and these hands-on exercises will challenge you to put theory into practice. Whether you're a Linux newcomer or a seasoned user looking to sharpen your skills, these exercises will provide valuable opportunities for experimentation, problem-solving, and creative exploration.

Grab your keyboard, open your terminal, and let's dive into these practical exercises to become a true Linux command line master!

5.1 Exercise 1: Navigating the File System

Objective: Practice navigating the Linux file system using various commands.

1. Open your terminal.

2. Use the **pwd** command to display the absolute path of your current working directory.

3. List the contents of your home directory using the **ls** command.

4. Move to the **Desktop** directory using the **cd** command.

5. List the contents of the **Desktop** directory.

6. Create a new directory called **Linux_Exercises** on your **Desktop**.

7. Move into the **Linux_Exercises** directory.

8. Create three new text files inside the **Linux_Exercises** directory: **file1.txt**, **file2.txt**, and **file3.txt**.

9. List the contents of the **Linux_Exercises** directory to confirm the files were created.

10. Rename **file1.txt** to **important_file.txt** using the **mv** command.

11. Move **important_file.txt** to your home directory.

12. Return to your home directory.

13. Use the **rm** command to remove **file2.txt** and **file3.txt** from the **Linux_Exercises** directory.

14. Remove the empty **Linux_Exercises** directory using the **rmdir** command.

5.2 Exercise 2: File Permissions

Objective: Practice changing file permissions and understanding their impact on access.

1. Create a new text file called **secret.txt** in your home directory.

2. Check the current permissions of **secret.txt** using the **ls -l** command.

3. Use the **chmod** command to set the permissions of **secret.txt** so that only the owner has read and write permissions, while the group and others have no permissions to read, write, or execute the file.

4. Verify that the permissions have been set correctly using the **ls -l** command.

5. Attempt to read the contents of **secret.txt** using a text editor. Note that you should not be able to read or modify the file.

6. Change the permissions of **secret.txt** so that the owner has read and write permissions, and the group and others have read-only permissions.

7. Verify that the permissions have been updated using the **ls -l** command.

8. Use a text editor to read and modify the contents of **secret.txt**. Note that you can read the file but cannot modify it.

5.3 Exercise 3: Text Processing

Objective: Practice text processing using Linux commands.

1. Create a new text file called **sample_text.txt** and write a few lines of text in it.

2. Use the **cat** command to display the contents of **sample_text.txt**.

3. Use the **grep** command to search for a specific word or phrase within **sample_text.txt**.

4. Use the **wc** command to count the number of lines, words, and characters in **sample_text.txt**.

5. Use the **sort** command to alphabetically sort the lines in **sample_text.txt**.

6. Use the **cut** command to extract specific columns from **sample_text.txt**.

7. Use the **sed** command to replace a word or phrase in **sample_text.txt** with another word or phrase.

8. Use the **head** command to display the first few lines of **sample_text.txt**.

9. Use the **tail** command to display the last few lines of **sample_text.txt**.

5.4 Exercise 4: File System Navigation Challenge

Objective: Practice navigating the file system efficiently using relative and absolute paths.

1. Start in your home directory.

2. Without using the **cd** command, navigate to the **Pictures** directory inside your home directory using the appropriate relative path.

3. List the contents of the **Pictures** directory to confirm you have successfully navigated to the correct location.

4. Navigate back to your home directory using an appropriate relative path.

5. Use an absolute path to move to the root directory.

6. From the root directory, navigate to the **Documents** directory inside your home directory using the appropriate absolute path.

7. List the contents of the **Documents** directory to ensure you have arrived at the correct location.

8. Return to your home directory using an appropriate relative path.

5.5 Exercise 5: File Management Challenge

Objective: Practice managing files and directories efficiently.

1. Create a new directory called **Linux_Backup** in your home directory.

2. Move all text files from the **Documents** directory to the **Linux_Backup** directory using the **mv** command.

3. List the contents of the **Linux_Backup** directory to ensure all text files have been moved successfully.

4. Rename the **Linux_Backup** directory to **Linux_Backup_YYYYMMDD**, replacing **YYYYMMDD** with today's date in the format year-month-day.

5. Use the **cp** command to create a copy of one of the text files from the **Linux_Backup_YYYYMMDD** directory and place it in your home directory.

6. List the contents of your home directory to confirm the copy was successful.

7. Create a new directory called **Temp** in your home directory.

8. Move the copied text file from your home directory to the **Temp** directory using the **mv** command.

9. List the contents of the **Temp** directory to verify the file has been moved.

10. Finally, delete the **Temp** directory along with its contents using the **rm** command.

5.6 Exercise 6: Advanced File Permissions

Objective: Practice setting advanced file permissions using symbolic notation.

1. Inside the **Confidential** directory, create two new text files: **confidential_data.txt** and **public_data.txt**.

2. Use the **chmod** command to set the permissions of **confidential_data.txt** so that only the owner has read and write permissions, and the group and others have no permissions to read, write, or execute the file.

3. Set the permissions of **public_data.txt** so that the owner, group, and others all have read and write permissions, but no execute permissions.

4. Use the **ls -l** command to verify that the permissions have been set correctly for both files.

5. Attempt to read the contents of both files using a text editor to test the permissions.

6. Change the permissions of **public_data.txt** to grant execute permissions to the owner, group, and others.

7. Use the **ls -l** command again to verify that the permissions have been updated for **public_data.txt**.

5.7 Exercise 7: Text Processing Challenge

Objective: Practice advanced text processing using Linux commands.

1. Create a new text file called **song_lyrics.txt** and write the lyrics of your favorite song in it.

2. Use the **cat** command to display the contents of **song_lyrics.txt**.

3. Use the **grep** command to search for a specific word or phrase within **song_lyrics.txt**.

4. Sort the lines in **song_lyrics.txt** alphabetically and save the sorted output to a new file called **sorted_lyrics.txt**.

5. Use the **cut** command to extract specific columns from **song_lyrics.txt** and save them to a new file called **chorus.txt**.

6. Use the **sed** command to replace a word or phrase in **song_lyrics.txt** with another word or phrase.

7. Display the first three lines of **song_lyrics.txt** using the **head** command.

8. Display the last three lines of **song_lyrics.txt** using the **tail** command.

9. Create a new directory called **Song_Stats** in your home directory.

10. Move the files **sorted_lyrics.txt** and **chorus.txt** to the **Song_Stats** directory using the **mv** command.

11. Finally, compress the **Song_Stats** directory into a zip file using the **zip** command.

5.8 Exercise 8: Shell Scripting Introduction

Objective: Practice creating and running simple shell scripts.

1. Open a text editor and create a new file called **greeting.sh**.

2. Write a shell script inside **greeting.sh** that greets the user with a personalized message based on their name. The script should prompt the user to enter their name and then display a greeting message like "Hello, [Name]! Welcome to the Linux world!".

3. Open your terminal and navigate to the directory where **greeting.sh** is located.

4. Run the shell script by executing the following command:

Copy code

bash greeting.sh

5. Follow the instructions and enter your name when prompted. Observe the personalized greeting displayed by the script.

6. Modify the shell script to include a check for an empty name entry. If the user enters an empty name, display a message like "You did not enter a name.

7. Save the changes to **greeting.sh** and run the script again to test the new functionality.

5.9 Exercise 9: Shell Scripting Automation

Objective: Practice automating repetitive tasks using shell scripts.

1. In your home directory, create a new directory called **Backup**.

2. Move all the text files from your **Documents** directory to the **Backup** directory using a shell script.

   - Check if the **Backup** directory exists. If not, create it.

   - Move all text files from **Documents** to **Backup**.

- Display a message indicating the number of files moved and their names.

3. Test the script by running it and confirming that the text files have been moved to the **Backup** directory.

4. Modify the script to include an automatic timestamp in the **Backup** directory's name. For example, the new directory should be named **Backup_YYYYMMDD_HHMMSS**.

5. Implement error handling in the script. If the **Documents** directory does not exist or there are no text files to move, display appropriate error messages.

6. Run the updated script and verify that it creates the timestamped **Backup** directory and moves the text files accordingly.

5.10 Exercise 10: Advanced Text Processing

Objective: Practice advanced text processing with pipelines and redirection.

1. Create a new text file called **sales_data.txt** and write several lines of sales data in the following format: **<Product Name>,<Quantity Sold>,<Unit Price>**. Separate each field with commas.

2. Use the **cat** command to display the contents of **sales_data.txt**.

3. Calculate the total revenue generated from each product sale using the **awk** command. Multiply the **Quantity Sold** by the **Unit Price** for each line and display the results.

4. Use the **grep** command to filter out specific product names from **sales_data.txt**. For example, display only the lines containing product names like "Laptop" or "Smartphone".

5. Create a new file called **summary.txt**. Redirect the output of the previous **awk** command to **summary.txt** to save the total revenue generated for each product.

6. Use the **sort** command to sort **summary.txt** in descending order based on total revenue.

7. Display the top 3 products with the highest revenue from **summary.txt** using the **head** command.

8. Finally, calculate the total revenue generated from all sales using the **awk** command, and display the result on the terminal.

Conclusion: Empowered with Practical Knowledge

Congratulations! By completing these practical exercises, you've gained valuable hands-on experience and reinforced your understanding of Linux concepts. You've navigated the file system, managed files and directories, manipulated file permissions, and processed text with confidence.

Remember that the best way to master Linux is through continuous practice and exploration. The Linux command line offers an endless array of possibilities and tools waiting for you to discover. So, keep experimenting, tackling real-world challenges, and building your Linux expertise.

In the next chapter, we'll explore additional advanced topics, such as shell scripting and automation, taking your Linux journey to even greater heights. Get ready for more exciting adventures in the world of Linux!

Happy learning and practicing!

CHAPTER 6

NETWORKING IN LINUX

Connecting and Securing Your Systems

Embracing the Network

Welcome to the exciting world of networking in Linux! In this chapter, we'll dive into the essential networking concepts that will empower you to connect your Linux systems to the world and ensure their security. Whether you're a Linux enthusiast, a system administrator, or a developer, understanding networking is fundamental for successful communication, data transfer, and collaboration in the digital age.

Linux, known for its robust networking capabilities, offers a wealth of tools and protocols to establish connections, configure networks, and safeguard your systems against potential threats. From basic network configurations to advanced security measures, we'll cover it all.

So, tighten your seatbelt, ready your terminal, and let's embark on a thrilling journey to explore the vast landscape of networking in Linux!

6.1 The Basics of Networking

Before delving into advanced topics, let's establish a strong foundation in networking.

Networking forms the backbone of modern computing, enabling devices to communicate, share resources, and access the internet. As we venture into the realm of Linux networking, it's essential to lay a robust foundation by understanding the fundamental concepts and terminologies.

73 6.1.1 IP Addressing and Subnetting

74 IP Addressing:

In the world of networking, devices need a unique identifier to communicate with each other. An IP (Internet Protocol) address serves as this identifier, enabling devices to send and receive data across networks.

75 IPv4:

For example, an IPv4 address might look like **192.168.1.100**. IPv4 allows for approximately 4.3 billion unique addresses, which were adequate in the early days of the internet but are now running out due to the exponential growth of connected devices.

76 IPv6:

To address the exhaustion of IPv4 addresses, IPv6 was introduced. IPv6 uses a 128-bit address format, expressed as eight groups of four hexadecimal digits separated by colons. For example, an IPv6 address looks like **2001:0db8:85a3:0000:0000:8a2e:0370:7334**. This format allows for an astronomical number of unique addresses, ensuring that we won't run out anytime soon.

77 Subnetting:

Subnetting is a technique used to divide a large IP address space into smaller, manageable sub-networks called subnets. Subnetting helps optimize address allocation, increase network efficiency, and enhance security.

78 Subnet Mask:

A subnet mask is a numeric value that determines the size of a subnet by designating which portion of an IP address represents the network and which part represents the host. It is typically written in the same format as the IP address, using bits set to 1 to represent the network portion and bits set to 0 to represent the host portion.

For example, with an IPv4 address of **192.168.1.100** and a subnet mask of **255.255.255.0**, the first three sets of numbers (**192.168.1**) represent the network, and the last set (**100**) represents the host.

79 6.1.2 Network Configuration

Network configuration involves setting up and managing network interfaces, defining IP addresses, configuring DNS (Domain Name System), and managing routing.

80   Network Interfaces:

In Linux, network interfaces are represented by names such as **eth0** or **enp0s3**. We'll learn how to view and manage network interfaces using tools like **ifconfig** and the newer **ip** command.

81   IP Address Configuration:

Assigning IP addresses to network interfaces is essential for communication. We'll explore different ways to configure IP addresses manually and automatically using DHCP (Dynamic Host Configuration Protocol).

82   DNS Configuration:

The Domain Name System (DNS) translates human-readable domain names (like example.com) into IP addresses. We'll learn how to configure DNS settings in Linux, enabling systems to resolve domain names and access websites.

83   Routing:

We'll explore how to view and manage routing tables in Linux, ensuring that data reaches its intended destination efficiently.

A Solid Networking Foundation

With a solid understanding of IP addressing, subnetting, network interfaces, and essential network configurations, you now possess a strong foundation in networking. These concepts are the building blocks of Linux networking, and they'll serve as a solid base as we dive into more advanced networking topics in the following chapters.

Networking is a fascinating and crucial aspect of modern computing, and Linux provides a wealth of tools and capabilities to create, configure, and manage networks effectively. So, buckle up as we explore the depths of Linux networking and take your connectivity to new heights!

84 6.1.1 IP Addressing and Subnetting

We'll learn about both IPv4 and IPv6 addressing schemes and how to configure IP addresses in Linux. Additionally, we'll explore subnetting to efficiently manage IP address spaces.

An IP (Internet Protocol) address plays a pivotal role in networking as it serves as a unique identifier assigned to each device connected to a network. Understanding IP addressing is fundamental for establishing communication between devices and facilitating data exchange.

85 IPv4 and IPv6 Addressing Schemes

86 IPv4 Addressing:

IPv4 (Internet Protocol version 4) addresses are the most widely used addresses on the internet today. They consist of 32 bits, usually represented in four groups of numbers separated by periods. Each group can range from 0 to 255. For example, an IPv4 address may look like **192.168.1.100**. IPv4 addresses were initially sufficient for the number of devices on the internet, but as the internet has grown exponentially, the available IPv4 address space is becoming depleted.

87 IPv6 Addressing:

To address the shortage of IPv4 addresses, IPv6 (Internet Protocol version 6) was introduced. IPv6 uses a 128-bit addressing scheme, expressed in eight groups of four hexadecimal digits, separated by colons. For example, an IPv6 address appears as **2001:0db8:85a3:0000:0000:8a2e:0370:7334**. This significantly larger address space in IPv6 allows for an enormous number of unique addresses, providing a virtually unlimited supply to accommodate the growing number of connected devices.

88 Configuring IP Addresses in Linux

In Linux, the process of configuring IP addresses can be accomplished manually or automatically, depending on the network requirements.

89 Manual Configuration:

To manually configure an IP address, you need to specify the IP address, subnet mask, and default gateway. The subnet mask determines which portion of the IP address represents the network and which part represents the host.

In Linux, you can use the **ifconfig** command to configure IP addresses. For example, to set the IP address of a network interface **eth0** to **192.168.1.100** with a subnet mask of **255.255.255.0**, you would use the following command:

Copy code

sudo ifconfig eth0 192.168.1.100 netmask 255.255.255.0

90 Automatic Configuration with DHCP:

Dynamic Host Configuration Protocol (DHCP) automates the process of IP address assignment. A DHCP server dynamically allocates IP addresses to devices on the network, making it easier to manage and administer large networks.

In Linux, you can use the **dhclient** command to obtain an IP address automatically from a DHCP server. For example:

Copy code

sudo dhclient eth0

91 Subnetting for Efficient IP Address Management

As networks grow in size, efficient IP address management becomes crucial. Subnetting is a technique used to divide a large IP address space into smaller sub-networks, known as subnets. Subnetting offers several benefits, including reduced network congestion, improved security, and simplified administration.

In subnetting, a subnet mask is used to distinguish the network portion from the host portion of an IP address. By customizing subnet masks, you can create smaller, manageable subnets.

For example, with an IP address like **192.168.1.100** and a subnet mask of **255.255.255.0**, the first three groups (**192.168.1**) represent the network, while the last group (**100**) identifies the host within that network.

By effectively subnetting, you can design network architectures that suit your specific needs, allowing for efficient use of IP addresses and more streamlined network management.

Conclusion: Empowering Network Communication

In this subsection, we've explored the fundamentals of IP addressing and the differences between IPv4 and IPv6. Additionally, we've learned how to configure IP addresses manually and automatically using DHCP in Linux. Understanding IP addressing and subnetting is crucial for establishing seamless network communication and ensuring that your devices can connect and communicate effectively.

In the next sections, we'll delve deeper into network configurations and explore various tools and commands that Linux offers to manage networks efficiently. Get ready to further enhance your networking knowledge and take control of your network infrastructure!

92 6.1.2 Network Configuration

Configuring network interfaces, setting up DNS (Domain Name System), and managing routing are crucial tasks in Linux. We'll explore tools like **ifconfig**, **ip**, and **route** to configure network settings effectively.

Configuring network interfaces, setting up DNS (Domain Name System), and managing routing are fundamental tasks in Linux networking. Proper network configuration is essential for enabling communication between devices and ensuring seamless data transfer.

93 Configuring Network Interfaces

A network interface is a hardware or software component that allows a device to connect to a network. In Linux, network interfaces are identified by names such as **eth0**, **enpOs3**, or **wlan0**. Configuring network interfaces involves assigning IP addresses, setting up subnet masks, and enabling or disabling interfaces.

94 Using **ifconfig**:

The **ifconfig** command has been a widely used tool for configuring network interfaces in Linux. It allows you to view and modify network interface settings, such as assigning an IP address, setting a subnet mask, enabling or disabling an interface, and configuring other parameters like the MTU (Maximum Transmission Unit).

For example, to set the IP address of **eth0** to **192.168.1.100** with a subnet mask of **255.255.255.0**, you would use the following command:

Copy code

```
sudo ifconfig eth0 192.168.1.100 netmask 255.255.255.0 up
```

95   The **ip** Command:

While **ifconfig** has been a longstanding tool, the **ip** command has become the modern replacement and offers more extensive functionality. It allows you to perform various network-related tasks, including configuring network interfaces, displaying routing tables, and managing the network stack.

To set the IP address of **eth0** to **192.168.1.100** with a subnet mask of **255.255.255.0**, you would use the following **ip** command:

csharpCopy code

```
sudo ip addr add 192.168.1.100/24 dev eth0
```

96 Setting Up DNS (Domain Name System)

DNS is a critical service that translates human-readable domain names, like **example.com**, into IP addresses that computers can understand. Configuring DNS settings in Linux allows your system to resolve domain names and access websites on the internet.

97 Editing **/etc/resolv.conf**:

The primary file for DNS configuration in Linux is **/etc/resolv.conf**. You can manually edit this file using a text editor to specify DNS servers, search domains, and other DNS-related parameters.

For example, to set Google's public DNS servers as your system's DNS resolvers, you would edit **/etc/resolv.conf** as follows:

Copy code

nameserver 8.8.8.8 nameserver 8.8.4.4

98 NetworkManager and **nmcli**:

Modern Linux distributions often use NetworkManager to manage network connections, including DNS settings. The **nmcli** command-line tool allows you to interact with NetworkManager and configure DNS settings easily.

99 Managing Routing

Routing is the process of directing network traffic from one network to another. Proper routing ensures that data packets reach their intended destination efficiently.

100 The **route** Command:

It allows you to add, delete, or modify routes manually.

For example, to add a route to the network **192.168.2.0** via the gateway **192.168.1.1** on interface **eth0**, you would use the following command:

csharpCopy code

```
sudo route add -net 192.168.2.0/24 gw 192.168.1.1 dev eth0
```

101 The **ip** Command for Routing:

Similarly to its versatility in network interface configuration, the **ip** command also provides functionalities for managing routing tables. You can add, delete, or modify routes using the **ip route** subcommand.

Efficient Network Configuration

In this subsection, we've explored the crucial aspects of network configuration in Linux. By understanding how to configure network interfaces, set up DNS settings, and manage routing, you can create efficient and reliable network connections.

The tools **ifconfig**, **ip**, and **route** play vital roles in configuring network settings effectively. Whether you're using the classic

ifconfig or embracing the versatility of **ip**, Linux offers the necessary tools to take full control of your network environment.

In the subsequent sections, we'll further delve into advanced networking topics, empowering you to build and manage robust networks in Linux. Get ready to embark on an exciting journey to enhance your networking prowess!

6.2 Establishing Network Connections

Connecting to networks and remote systems is a common scenario in Linux. We'll explore various protocols and tools to establish secure connections.

In the world of Linux, establishing network connections is a common and essential task. Whether you need to connect to a local network, access resources on remote systems, or communicate securely with other devices, Linux offers a wide range of protocols and tools to facilitate these connections.

1026.2.1 SSH (Secure Shell)

103 Introduction to SSH:

SSH (Secure Shell) is a cryptographic network protocol that provides secure communication over a network. It allows users to access and manage remote systems securely, making it a fundamental tool for system administrators and developers.

104 Establishing SSH Connections:

To establish an SSH connection to a remote system, you'll need the remote system's IP address or domain name, as well as valid login credentials. The most common tool for SSH is the **ssh** command.

To connect to a remote system via SSH, use the following syntax:

cssCopy code

ssh username@remote_ip_or_domain

For example, to connect to a remote system with the username **john** and the IP address **192.168.1.100**, you would use:

cssCopy code

ssh john@192.168.1.100

105 Key-Based Authentication:

SSH also supports key-based authentication, which provides a more secure and convenient way to connect to remote systems without entering passwords. Key-based authentication involves generating a key pair consisting of a public key and a private key. The public key is placed on the remote system, while the private key is kept on your local machine.

Copy code

ssh-keygen

Once the key pair is generated, you can copy the public key to the remote system's **~/.ssh/authorized_keys** file to enable key-based authentication.

1066.2.2 FTP (File Transfer Protocol) and SFTP (SSH File Transfer Protocol)

107 FTP:

FTP (File Transfer Protocol) is a standard network protocol used for transferring files between a client and a server on a network. While FTP is a convenient way to transfer files, it lacks security mechanisms, making it unsuitable for sensitive data transfer over untrusted networks.

108 SFTP:

SFTP (SSH File Transfer Protocol) is a secure extension of FTP that uses SSH to encrypt and secure file transfers. SFTP provides all the functionality of traditional FTP but with the added benefit of encryption, ensuring data privacy during transmission.

109 Establishing SFTP Connections:

To establish an SFTP connection to a remote server, you can use the **sftp** command, similar to SSH.

To connect to a remote system via SFTP, use the following syntax:

cssCopy code

sftp username@remote_ip_or_domain

For example, to connect to an SFTP server with the username **john** and the IP address **192.168.1.100**, you would use:

cssCopy code

sftp john@192.168.1.100

1106.2.3 HTTP/HTTPS

111 Introduction to HTTP/HTTPS:

It facilitates the exchange of information between a client (typically a web browser) and a web server. While HTTP is widely used, it lacks security features, leaving transmitted data vulnerable to interception and manipulation.

HTTPS (Hypertext Transfer Protocol Secure) is the secure version of HTTP, using encryption to protect data during transmission. HTTPS is commonly used for secure online transactions, sensitive data transfer, and secure browsing.

112 Browsing with HTTP/HTTPS:

To access websites using HTTP or HTTPS, you can use web browsers like Firefox, Chrome, or Chromium. Simply enter the website's URL in the browser's address bar, and the browser will initiate an HTTP or HTTPS connection to the web server.

Secure and Seamless Networking

In this section, we've explored different protocols and tools to establish secure and seamless network connections in Linux. Whether you need to connect to remote systems via SSH, transfer files securely with SFTP, or browse the web using HTTP or HTTPS, Linux offers a diverse range of solutions to meet your networking needs.

As you continue your Linux journey, mastering these networking tools will empower you to navigate the vast digital landscape with confidence, ensuring secure communication and efficient data transfer across networks. So, embrace the power of Linux networking and unlock endless possibilities for seamless connectivity!

1136.2.1 SSH (Secure Shell)

SSH is a secure and encrypted protocol widely used for remote access and command execution. We'll learn how to use SSH to connect to remote systems securely and perform administrative tasks.

SSH (Secure Shell) is a powerful and widely-used cryptographic network protocol that provides secure and encrypted communication over a network. It is a fundamental tool in the Linux world, offering a secure method for remote access and command execution on remote systems. SSH is not only essential for system administrators and developers but also for anyone who needs secure access to remote resources.

114Introduction to SSH

SSH is designed to replace insecure remote access protocols like Telnet and rlogin, which transmitted data in plaintext, leaving it vulnerable to interception and unauthorized access. SSH, on the other hand, encrypts all data exchanged between the client and the server, providing a secure channel for communication.

One of the key features of SSH is its ability to authenticate users securely using various methods, including password-based authentication and key-based authentication. The latter involves using a key pair, consisting of a public key and a private key, to authenticate the user.

115Establishing SSH Connections

To establish an SSH connection to a remote system, you need the remote system's IP address or domain name, as well as valid login credentials (username and password). If you're using key-based authentication, you'll also need the corresponding private key.

116 Using the **ssh** Command

The most common tool for establishing SSH connections is the **ssh** command, which comes pre-installed on most Linux distributions.

To connect to a remote system via SSH, use the following syntax:

cssCopy code

ssh username@remote_ip_or_domain

For example, to connect to a remote system with the username **john** and the IP address **192.168.1.100**, you would use:

cssCopy code

ssh john@192.168.1.100

If you're using key-based authentication, you can specify the private key file with the **-i** option:

cssCopy code

ssh -i /path/to/private_key username@remote_ip_or_domain

117 Key-Based Authentication

Key-based authentication is more secure and convenient than password-based authentication. It involves generating a key pair on your local machine, where the private key is kept, and copying the public key to the remote system's **~/.ssh/authorized_keys** file.

Copy code

ssh-keygen

The public key is usually stored in the file **~/.ssh/id_rsa.pub**, and the private key is stored in **~/.ssh/id_rsa**. You can copy the public key to the remote system using the **ssh-copy-id** command:

sqlCopy code

ssh-copy-id username@remote_ip_or_domain

Once the public key is added to the remote system's **~/.ssh/authorized_keys** file, you can connect to the remote system using key-based authentication without entering a password.

118Performing Administrative Tasks with SSH

SSH provides a secure command-line interface to the remote system, allowing you to perform various administrative tasks, execute commands, transfer files, and manage the system remotely. This makes SSH an indispensable tool for system administrators and anyone needing remote access to a Linux machine.

For example, you can execute a command remotely on the remote system using SSH like this:

bashCopy code

ssh username@remote_ip_or_domain command

This will execute the specified command on the remote system and display the output on your local terminal.

Conclusion: Secure Remote Access with SSH

In this subsection, we've explored the power and versatility of SSH as a secure and encrypted protocol for remote access and command execution in Linux. SSH's ability to authenticate users securely, combined with its encrypted communication, ensures that sensitive data and login credentials are protected from unauthorized access and interception.

By mastering SSH, you can securely connect to remote systems, perform administrative tasks, and manage resources with confidence. As you continue your Linux journey, SSH will prove to be an indispensable tool in your arsenal, enabling seamless remote access and secure communication across networks. Embrace the security and convenience of SSH and unlock the true potential of remote administration in Linux.

1196.2.2 FTP (File Transfer Protocol) and SFTP (SSH File Transfer Protocol)

FTP and SFTP are used for transferring files between systems. We'll compare both protocols, explore their differences, and learn how to use them for file transfer.

FTP (File Transfer Protocol) and SFTP (SSH File Transfer Protocol) are both widely used for transferring files between systems. However, they have distinct characteristics, including their security features and the methods they use for data transmission. Let's delve into the comparison between these two protocols, explore their differences, and learn how to use them for efficient and secure file transfer.

120 FTP (File Transfer Protocol)

121 Introduction to FTP

FTP is one of the earliest network protocols developed for file transfer, and it remains widely used to this day. It operates on two separate channels: the command channel (control channel) and the data channel. The command channel is responsible for sending commands and receiving responses, while the data channel is used for actual file transfer.

122 FTP Features

FTP allows for easy file transfer between a client and a server. It supports various commands for listing files, navigating directories, uploading, and downloading files. FTP is relatively straightforward to use, making it accessible for users of all levels of technical expertise.

123 Security Concerns

However, one significant drawback of FTP is its lack of built-in security features. Data transmitted via FTP is not encrypted, leaving it vulnerable to interception by unauthorized parties.

Because of this inherent security flaw, FTP is not recommended for transferring sensitive or confidential data over untrusted networks, such as the internet.

124 SFTP (SSH File Transfer Protocol)

125 Introduction to SFTP

SFTP, on the other hand, is a secure extension of FTP that operates over an SSH (Secure Shell) connection. Unlike traditional FTP, SFTP encrypts all data during transmission, providing a secure channel for file transfer. It benefits from the strong security features of SSH, making it suitable for secure file transfer even over untrusted networks.

126 SFTP Features

SFTP offers similar functionality to FTP, supporting commands for listing files, navigating directories, and transferring files between the client and the server. Since it operates over SSH, SFTP also provides additional features like remote file editing and file attribute manipulation.

127 Enhanced Security

One of the significant advantages of SFTP is its enhanced security. All data, including login credentials and file contents, is encrypted, protecting it from interception and unauthorized access. As a result, SFTP is the preferred choice when security is a priority, especially for transferring sensitive data and confidential files.

128Using FTP and SFTP for File Transfer

129 FTP Client Usage

To connect to an FTP server and transfer files, you can use various FTP clients, such as **ftp** or **FileZilla**.

For example, to connect to an FTP server using the **ftp** command, you would use the following syntax:

Copy code

```
ftp ftp_server_ip_or_domain
```

After connecting, you can use FTP commands like **ls**, **get**, **put**, and **cd** to list files, download files, upload files, and navigate directories.

130 SFTP Client Usage

SFTP clients, such as **sftp**, **WinSCP**, or **FileZilla**, are used to connect to an SFTP server and perform secure file transfers.

To connect to an SFTP server using the **sftp** command, you would use the following syntax:

cssCopy code

```
sftp username@remote_ip_or_domain
```

Once connected, you can use SFTP commands like **ls**, **get**, **put**, and **cd** similar to FTP, but with the added benefit of secure, encrypted data transfer.

Choosing the Right Protocol for File Transfer

In this subsection, we've compared FTP and SFTP, highlighting their distinct features and security considerations. While FTP remains a simple and straightforward choice for basic file transfer, it lacks the security necessary for sensitive data transmission.

On the other hand, SFTP provides robust security through its encryption capabilities, making it the preferred option for secure file transfer. When handling sensitive data or transferring files over untrusted networks, SFTP is the recommended protocol.

As you continue your journey in Linux, consider the nature of your file transfer needs and prioritize security when selecting between FTP and SFTP. Embrace the convenience and security of SFTP to ensure safe and efficient file transfer between systems.

1316.2.3 HTTP/HTTPS

HTTP and HTTPS are essential for web browsing and server-client communication. We'll understand the principles behind web servers, learn how to host a website, and explore security measures for HTTPS connections.

HTTP (Hypertext Transfer Protocol) and its secure counterpart HTTPS (Hypertext Transfer Protocol Secure) are fundamental protocols for web browsing and server-client communication. Understanding the principles behind web servers and learning how to host a website will empower you to take your online presence to new heights. Additionally, we'll explore the security measures that HTTPS provides, ensuring safe and encrypted data transmission between clients and servers.

132 Web Servers and HTTP

133 Introduction to Web Servers

Web servers are software applications responsible for processing incoming HTTP requests from clients (web browsers) and responding with the requested web pages. They store and serve web content, such as HTML, CSS, JavaScript, and multimedia files, to users who access websites through their web browsers.

134 HTTP Basics

When you type a URL into your web browser and press Enter, your browser sends an HTTP request to the web server hosting that website. The web server processes the request and responds with the requested web page, which your browser then renders and displays.

HTTP is designed around the client-server model, where clients (web browsers) make requests to servers, and servers respond with the requested data.

135 Hosting a Website with HTTP

136 Steps to Host a Website

To host a website, you'll need a web server software, such as Apache, Nginx, or Lighttpd, installed on your server. You'll also need to configure your web server to serve the website's files and respond to incoming HTTP requests.

Here are some basic steps to host a website using Apache as an example:

1. Install Apache:

sqlCopy code

sudo apt update sudo apt install apache2

2. Place website files: Upload your website's files (HTML, CSS, JavaScript, etc.) to the appropriate directory on the server, usually under **/var/www/html/**.

3. Configure virtual hosts: If hosting multiple websites on the same server, set up virtual hosts to differentiate between them.

4. Enable the website:

Copy code

sudo a2ensite your_website.conf

5. Restart Apache:

Copy code

sudo systemctl restart apache2

Your website should now be accessible via its domain name or IP address.

137 HTTPS and Secure Communication

138 Introduction to HTTPS

It uses SSL/TLS protocols to encrypt data transmitted between the client and the server, protecting it from eavesdropping and manipulation by attackers.

139 How HTTPS Works

When you connect to a website via HTTPS, your web browser and the web server establish an encrypted SSL/TLS connection. This is done using digital certificates, which verify the authenticity of the server and establish a secure channel for data exchange.

140 Securing Web Traffic with HTTPS

141 Obtaining an SSL Certificate

To enable HTTPS for your website, you'll need an SSL certificate issued by a trusted Certificate Authority (CA). You can obtain SSL certificates for free from Let's Encrypt or purchase them from commercial CAs.

142 Configuring HTTPS on Apache

Once you have an SSL certificate, you can configure Apache to use HTTPS. This involves modifying the virtual host configuration to specify the SSL certificate and private key.

Here are the basic steps to enable HTTPS on Apache:

1. Install Certbot (Let's Encrypt client):

Copy code

```
sudo apt install certbot python3-certbot-apache
```

2. Obtain the SSL certificate and enable HTTPS for your website:

cssCopy code

```
sudo certbot --apache -d your_domain.com
```

3. Restart Apache:

Copy code

```
sudo systemctl restart apache2
```

Your website should now be accessible via HTTPS, providing encrypted and secure communication between clients and your web server.

Power of HTTP/HTTPS

In this subsection, we've explored the crucial role of HTTP and HTTPS in web browsing and server-client communication. Web servers facilitate the delivery of web content, while HTTP ensures data exchange between clients and servers. Hosting a website involves setting up a web server and configuring it to serve website files.

However, when it comes to sensitive data and secure communication, HTTPS takes the lead. It provides encryption and ensures safe data transmission, making it vital for protecting user information, login credentials, and sensitive transactions.

As you navigate the digital realm, remember the importance of HTTPS in safeguarding data and enabling secure web communication. Embrace HTTPS to build trust with your users and create a secure online experience for your website visitors.

6.3 Network Security and Firewalls

Securing your Linux systems from unauthorized access and potential threats is paramount. We'll explore network security measures and firewalls to protect your systems.

Securing your Linux systems from unauthorized access and potential threats is of utmost importance in today's interconnected world. Network security measures and firewalls play a critical role in protecting your systems from malicious activities and safeguarding sensitive data. In this subsection, we'll explore the fundamentals of network security and the vital role of firewalls in fortifying your Linux environment.

143 Understanding Network Security

144 Network Security Essentials

Network security encompasses a range of practices and technologies designed to protect the integrity, confidentiality, and availability of data and resources within a network. It involves the implementation of various security measures to prevent unauthorized access, data breaches, and other potential security threats.

Key aspects of network security include:

1. **Authentication and Access Control**: Implementing strong authentication methods and access controls to ensure that only authorized users have access to specific resources.

2. **Encryption**: Utilizing encryption techniques to protect data during transmission and storage, making it unreadable to unauthorized entities.

3. **Intrusion Detection and Prevention**: Employing intrusion detection systems (IDS) and intrusion prevention systems (IPS) to monitor network traffic and detect and block suspicious activities.

4. **Network Monitoring and Logging**: Regularly monitoring network activity and maintaining detailed logs to identify potential security incidents and facilitate post-incident analysis.

5. **Patch Management**: Keeping operating systems and software up-to-date with the latest security patches to address known vulnerabilities.

145 Firewalls: The Guardians of Network Security

146 What is a Firewall?

It inspects incoming and outgoing network traffic and applies predefined rules to permit or block specific data packets based on security policies.

147 Firewall Types and Functionality

There are two primary types of firewalls:

1. **Packet Filtering Firewalls**: These firewalls examine individual data packets and make decisions to allow or deny their passage based on specific criteria, such as source and destination IP addresses, port numbers, and protocol types.

2. **Stateful Inspection Firewalls**: Stateful firewalls maintain information about active connections and use this context to make more intelligent decisions about which packets to allow or deny. They offer better security and are more resistant to certain types of attacks.

148 Configuring Firewalls on Linux

Linux systems often come with built-in firewall software called **iptables** (legacy) or **nftables** (modern). These tools allow you to configure packet filtering rules and manage network traffic effectively.

To create a basic rule in **iptables** to allow incoming SSH connections, you would use the following command:

In **nftables**, the equivalent command would be:

cssCopy code

sudo nft add rule ip filter input tcp dport 22 accept

149 Conclusion: Fortify Your Network

In this subsection, we've explored the critical role of network security and firewalls in protecting your Linux systems from potential threats and unauthorized access. Network security measures, such as encryption and access control, are essential for maintaining the integrity and confidentiality of your data.

Firewalls act as the guardians of your network, filtering and controlling network traffic based on predefined rules. By configuring firewalls on your Linux systems, you can effectively control incoming and outgoing network communication, bolstering your defenses against malicious activities.

Remember, network security is an ongoing process that requires vigilance and regular updates to adapt to evolving threats. By prioritizing network security and staying informed about the latest best practices, you can fortify your Linux environment and ensure a safe and secure computing experience for yourself and your users.

1506.3.1 Firewalls and iptables

Firewalls are a vital defense mechanism. We'll delve into **iptables**, a powerful firewall tool in Linux, and learn how to configure rules to control network traffic effectively.

Firewalls serve as vital defense mechanisms in protecting your Linux systems from unauthorized access and potential threats. Among the various firewall tools available in Linux, **iptables** stands out as a powerful and versatile solution. In this subsection, we'll delve into the world of **iptables** and learn how to configure rules to control network traffic effectively, enhancing the security of your Linux environment.

151Understanding iptables

152 What is **iptables**?

iptables is a user-space utility in Linux that allows you to set up and manage firewall rules for IPv4 packets. It acts as a packet filtering firewall, examining incoming and outgoing network packets and making decisions about whether to allow or deny them based on defined rules.

153 **iptables** Components

iptables consists of various components, including:

1. **Chains**: These are predefined sets of rules that determine how packets should be processed. The three default chains are INPUT (incoming packets), OUTPUT (outgoing packets), and FORWARD (packets being forwarded between interfaces).

2. **Rules**: Each rule specifies criteria that packets must match for the action (ACCEPT, DROP, REJECT, etc.) to be applied. Rules are organized in chains and are evaluated in order from the top down.

3. **Tables**: **iptables** uses different tables to hold rules. The four main tables are filter (default table for packet filtering), nat (for network address translation), mangle (for specialized packet alteration), and raw (for bypassing connection tracking).

154 Working with **iptables**

Configuring **iptables** involves adding, modifying, or deleting rules within specific chains and tables. The typical workflow for using **iptables** involves the following steps:

1. **Viewing Existing Rules**: To see the current **iptables** rules, use the following command:

Copy code

sudo iptables -L

2. **Adding Rules**: To add a new rule, you specify the chain, the rule criteria, and the action. For example, to allow incoming SSH connections, you would use:

3. **Modifying and Deleting Rules**: To modify or delete existing rules, use the **-R** and **-D** options, respectively.

4. **Saving Rules**: To save your **iptables** rules to persist across reboots, you can use the **iptables-persistent** package (Ubuntu/Debian) or **iptables-save** and **iptables-restore** commands.

155 Configuring iptables for Network Traffic Control

156 Example: Allowing SSH and HTTP Traffic

Let's create an example **iptables** rule set to allow incoming SSH and HTTP traffic while blocking all other incoming connections.

1. Allow SSH (port 22) connections:

2. Allow HTTP (port 80) connections:

3. Drop all other incoming connections:

cssCopy code

sudo iptables -A INPUT -j DROP

Harnessing the Power of iptables

In this subsection, we've explored the significance of firewalls and introduced **iptables** as a robust packet filtering firewall tool in Linux. With **iptables**, you can craft specific rules to control network traffic effectively, allowing you to fortify your Linux environment against potential threats.

By understanding the components and workflow of **iptables**, you gain the ability to fine-tune the security of your system and ensure that only authorized traffic is allowed while blocking malicious attempts.

Remember, **iptables** is just one aspect of network security, and a comprehensive security strategy involves considering other measures such as access controls, encryption, and regular system updates. By incorporating **iptables** into your security arsenal, you enhance the overall defense of your Linux systems, making them more resilient against unauthorized access and potential risks.

1576.3.2 VPN (Virtual Private Network)

VPN provides a secure and encrypted connection between remote systems. We'll understand how VPNs work, explore different types of VPNs, and set up a VPN server on Linux.

Virtual Private Network (VPN) technology offers a secure and encrypted connection between remote systems, making it a valuable tool for enhancing network security and privacy. In this subsection, we'll dive into the world of VPNs, understand how they work, explore different types of VPNs, and learn how to set up a VPN server on Linux.

158Understanding VPNs

159 What is a VPN?

A Virtual Private Network (VPN) creates a private and secure communication tunnel over a public network, such as the internet. It allows users to access resources and services securely as if they were directly connected to a private network, even if they are geographically distant.

160 How VPNs Work

VPNs work by encrypting data transmitted between a client and a VPN server. When a user connects to a VPN, their data travels through the encrypted tunnel, ensuring that any information intercepted by potential attackers remains unreadable and unusable.

By masking the user's IP address with the VPN server's IP address, VPNs also provide a level of anonymity and prevent websites and services from tracking the user's actual location.

161 Types of VPNs

162 1. Remote Access VPNs:

Remote Access VPNs allow individual users to connect securely to a private network from a remote location. This is particularly useful for employees accessing corporate resources while working from home or traveling.

163 2. Site-to-Site VPNs:

Site-to-Site VPNs (also known as Router-to-Router VPNs) connect entire networks together, enabling secure communication between multiple locations. This is commonly used in businesses with branch offices, allowing them to share resources securely.

164 3. Point-to-Point Tunneling Protocol (PPTP):

PPTP is an older and less secure VPN protocol that was widely used in the past. It offers relatively easy setup but has known vulnerabilities and is not recommended for secure connections.

165 4. Layer 2 Tunneling Protocol (L2TP):

L2TP is another VPN protocol that provides more security than PPTP. It is often used in combination with IPsec (Internet Protocol Security) to enhance encryption and data integrity.

166 5. OpenVPN:

OpenVPN is a popular and highly regarded open-source VPN protocol known for its strong security features and flexibility. It can be used with both TCP and UDP protocols and is supported on various platforms.

167 Setting Up a VPN Server on Linux

168 Using OpenVPN

OpenVPN is a versatile and reliable option for setting up a VPN server on Linux.

Install OpenVPN: Install the OpenVPN package on your Linux server.

1. **Generate Certificates and Keys**: Generate SSL certificates and keys for authentication and encryption.

2. **Configure OpenVPN**: Create an OpenVPN configuration file, specifying server settings, encryption options, and client authentication details.

3. **Enable IP Forwarding**: Enable IP forwarding on your server to allow traffic to pass through the VPN tunnel.

4. **Firewall Configuration**: Configure your firewall to allow VPN traffic.

5. **Start OpenVPN**: Start the OpenVPN service to launch the VPN server.

Embracing the Security of VPNs

In this subsection, we've explored the power and security benefits of Virtual Private Networks (VPNs). VPNs play a crucial role in securing communication and data transmission over public networks, making them an essential tool for both individuals and businesses.

By understanding how VPNs work and the different types available, you can choose the best VPN solution to meet your specific needs. Setting up a VPN server on Linux using OpenVPN provides you with a robust and customizable option for establishing a secure and encrypted communication channel.

Remember, VPNs are not a one-size-fits-all solution, and careful consideration of security, performance, and usability factors is crucial when implementing a VPN solution. By embracing the security and privacy that VPNs offer, you can confidently navigate the digital realm, knowing that your data and communication are shielded from potential threats and unauthorized access.

6.4 Troubleshooting Network Issues

Networking isn't always smooth sailing. We'll equip you with troubleshooting techniques to identify and resolve common network issues.

Networking can be complex, and even in the best-configured systems, issues may arise. Don't worry; we'll equip you with troubleshooting techniques to help you identify and resolve common network issues efficiently. By following these steps, you can become a network problem-solving pro.

169 Step 1: Check Physical Connections

The first step in troubleshooting network issues is to inspect the physical connections. Faulty or disconnected cables can lead to network interruptions.

170 Step 2: Verify IP Configuration

Check the IP configuration of the affected device. Incorrect IP addresses, subnet masks, or gateway settings can cause connectivity problems. Use the **ipconfig** command on Windows or the **ifconfig** command on Linux to view and validate the network settings.

171 Step 3: Ping Test

Perform a ping test to check if there is connectivity between devices. A successful ping indicates that the devices can communicate with each other.

172 Step 4: Check DNS Settings

If you're having trouble accessing websites, the issue might be related to DNS (Domain Name System). Verify that your DNS settings are correct, or try using public DNS servers like Google's (8.8.8.8 and 8.8.4.4) to see if the problem persists.

173Step 5: Disable Firewall and Antivirus

Sometimes, overzealous firewall or antivirus software can block legitimate network traffic. Temporarily disable these security programs to see if they are causing the issue. If the problem resolves, reconfigure the firewall or antivirus settings to allow necessary network traffic.

174Step 6: Restart Networking Devices

Restart your modem, router, and switches to clear any temporary glitches. Power cycling these devices can often resolve network issues caused by device hang-ups.

175Step 7: Check Network Logs

Examine network logs on routers, switches, and servers to identify potential errors or abnormal activities. Logs can provide valuable clues about the source of network issues.

176Step 8: Use Network Troubleshooting Tools

Network troubleshooting tools can simplify the process of identifying and diagnosing network problems. Tools like **ping**, **traceroute**, and **nslookup** can help pinpoint connectivity and DNS-related issues.

177 Step 9: Perform Loopback Tests

Loopback tests involve connecting a device to itself to check if its network interface is functioning correctly. This can help identify hardware issues with network adapters or drivers.

178 Step 10: Check for Network Congestion

High network traffic or congestion can cause slow performance. Check for bandwidth-intensive applications or devices that may be overwhelming the network. Consider Quality of Service (QoS) settings to prioritize critical traffic.

179 Step 11: Update Firmware and Drivers

Outdated firmware on routers or outdated network drivers on devices can cause compatibility issues. Check for updates and apply the latest firmware and driver releases.

180 Step 12: Seek Professional Assistance

If all else fails and you cannot identify or resolve the network issue, don't hesitate to seek professional assistance. Network administrators or IT support teams can offer specialized expertise to tackle more complex problems.

181 Conclusion: Mastering Network Troubleshooting

In this subsection, we've equipped you with essential network troubleshooting techniques to overcome common network issues. By following these steps and employing network troubleshooting tools, you can efficiently diagnose and resolve connectivity problems, ensuring a smooth and reliable network experience.

Remember, network troubleshooting is a valuable skill that comes with experience and persistence. Keep honing your troubleshooting skills, and you'll become a network-savvy troubleshooter capable of resolving a wide range of networking challenges.

1826.4.1 Ping and Traceroute

ping and **traceroute** are valuable tools for diagnosing connectivity problems and tracing network paths. We'll use them to diagnose network issues effectively.

Ping and traceroute are invaluable network diagnostic tools that play a crucial role in identifying connectivity problems and tracing the path of network packets. By using these tools effectively, you can diagnose network issues and gain insights into the health and performance of your network.

183 Ping: Testing Connectivity

184 What is Ping?

Ping is a basic network utility used to test the reachability of a device or host on a network. It sends small packets of data to the target device and measures the time it takes for the packets to travel back, known as round-trip time (RTT).

185 Using Ping

phpCopy code

ping <target_device_or_host>

For example, to ping Google's public DNS server (8.8.8.8), you would enter:

Copy code

ping 8.8.8.8

186 Interpreting Ping Results

A successful ping test shows the response time (in milliseconds) for each packet sent. If packets are reaching the target device and returning, the ping results will show the round-trip time.

A high ping time or "Request timed out" messages indicate potential connectivity issues. Consistently high ping times may suggest network congestion or server problems.

187 Traceroute: Tracing Network Paths

188 What is Traceroute?

Traceroute is a tool that traces the route that packets take from your device to a target host or IP address. It displays a list of the routers or "hops" the packets travel through, showing the time it takes to reach each router.

189 Using Traceroute

phpCopy code

traceroute <target_host_or_ip>

For example, to trace the route to Google's website (www.google.com), you would enter:

Copy code

traceroute www.google.com

190 Interpreting Traceroute Results

Traceroute displays the IP addresses of the routers (or hops) along the path to the target. The round-trip times for each hop indicate the time it takes for packets to travel to that router and back.

By examining traceroute results, you can identify the path packets take and pinpoint potential network bottlenecks or points of failure.

Harnessing Ping and Traceroute for Troubleshooting

In this subsection, we've explored the power of ping and traceroute as essential network diagnostic tools. Ping helps test the connectivity between devices, while traceroute allows us to trace the path packets take through the network.

By utilizing ping and traceroute effectively, you can diagnose connectivity issues, measure network performance, and identify potential areas of concern. These tools play a vital role in network troubleshooting and provide valuable insights into the health and efficiency of your network.

As you continue to refine your network troubleshooting skills, mastering the use of ping and traceroute will empower you to tackle network issues with confidence and precision, ensuring a robust and reliable network experience.

1916.4.2 Network Diagnostics and Tools

We'll explore various network diagnostic tools, such as **netstat**, **tcpdump**, and **wireshark**, to monitor network traffic, analyze packets, and identify potential anomalies.

In addition to ping and traceroute, there are several other powerful network diagnostic tools available that can help you monitor network traffic, analyze packets, and identify potential anomalies. Let's explore some of these tools and their capabilities.

192Netstat: Network Statistics

193 What is Netstat?

Netstat (Network Statistics) is a command-line tool that provides detailed information about network connections, routing tables, interface statistics, and more.

194 Using Netstat

To use netstat, open a command prompt or terminal and type:

cssCopy code

netstat [options]

For example, to display all active network connections, you would enter:

cssCopy code

netstat -a

195 Interpreting Netstat Results

Netstat displays information such as active connections, listening ports, and the state of network connections. It can help you identify which ports are in use, which processes are associated with specific connections, and detect any suspicious or unexpected network activities.

196 Tcpdump: Packet Capture and Analysis

197 What is Tcpdump?

Tcpdump is a powerful packet capture and analysis tool used to capture network traffic in real-time. It captures packets and can save them to a file for later analysis.

198 Using Tcpdump

To use tcpdump, open a command prompt or terminal and type:

cssCopy code

tcpdump [options]

For example, to capture packets on a specific network interface, you would enter:

cssCopy code

tcpdump -i eth0

199 Interpreting Tcpdump Results

Tcpdump captures packets and displays information such as source and destination IP addresses, protocol types, port numbers, and packet payloads. By analyzing the captured packets, you can diagnose network issues, monitor for suspicious activity, and gain insights into network traffic patterns.

200 Wireshark: Network Protocol Analyzer

201 What is Wireshark?

Wireshark is a popular and user-friendly network protocol analyzer that allows you to capture and examine packets in a graphical interface. It offers in-depth analysis of network traffic and supports various protocols.

202 Using Wireshark

To use Wireshark, download and install it on your system. Once installed, open Wireshark and select the network interface you wish to capture packets from. Click "Start" to begin capturing packets.

203 Interpreting Wireshark Results

Wireshark provides a detailed view of captured packets, allowing you to inspect individual packets, filter traffic based on specific criteria, and analyze network behavior at a granular level. It is particularly useful for troubleshooting complex network issues and identifying the root cause of problems.

Enhancing Network Diagnostics with Advanced Tools

In this subsection, we've explored advanced network diagnostic tools, including netstat, tcpdump, and Wireshark. These tools provide detailed insights into network connections, real-time packet capture, and protocol analysis.

By harnessing these tools effectively, you can monitor network performance, detect anomalies, troubleshoot connectivity issues, and maintain a secure and efficient network environment.

As you delve into the world of advanced network diagnostics, remember to use these tools responsibly and be mindful of privacy and security concerns. Continuous learning and practice with these diagnostic tools will empower you to become a proficient network administrator, ensuring optimal network performance and safeguarding against potential threats.

Conclusion: A Connected and Secure Linux World

Congratulations on expanding your knowledge of networking in Linux! You've gained the necessary skills to configure networks, establish secure connections, and protect your systems from potential threats.

Networking is a crucial aspect of the digital landscape, enabling seamless communication and data exchange. Armed with the knowledge and tools from this chapter, you're now better equipped to navigate the intricacies of networking in Linux.

In the next chapter, we'll dive into advanced system administration, covering topics such as process management, resource monitoring, and performance optimization. Get ready to level up your Linux administration skills!

Keep exploring, keep learning, and continue to embrace the connected and secure world of Linux networking!

CHAPTER 7

SYSTEM ADMINISTRATION

ESSENTIALS

Taking Charge of Your Linux Environment

Welcome to Chapter 7 of our comprehensive guide, where we delve into the realm of System Administration Essentials. In this chapter, we will equip you with the necessary skills to take charge of your Linux environment, enabling you to manage and optimize it effectively. System administration is a crucial aspect of maintaining a healthy and well-functioning Linux system, and understanding the core concepts and practical techniques will empower you to become a proficient Linux administrator.

204Understanding System Administration

205 The Role of a System Administrator

System administrators, often referred to as sysadmins, play a vital role in managing and maintaining Linux systems. They are responsible for tasks such as installation, configuration, monitoring, troubleshooting, security, and overall system optimization. A skilled sysadmin ensures that the Linux environment runs smoothly, provides reliable services, and remains secure from potential threats.

206 System Administration Principles

Before diving into specific tasks, let's explore some key principles of effective system administration:

1. **Proactive Monitoring**: Regularly monitoring system resources, performance metrics, and log files helps identify potential issues before they escalate.

2. **Automation**: Embracing automation with tools like shell scripts and configuration management systems streamlines repetitive tasks and enhances system efficiency.

3. **Documentation**: Thorough and up-to-date documentation is essential for tracking configurations, changes, and troubleshooting steps.

4. **Security Best Practices**: Implementing security measures, such as user access controls, firewalls, and timely updates, ensures system integrity and data protection.

207 Essential System Administration Tasks

208 1. User and Group Management

Managing users and groups is fundamental to controlling access to your Linux environment. Creating, modifying, and deleting user accounts, as well as assigning proper permissions, are essential tasks for maintaining system security and organizing user privileges.

209 2. File System Management

Understanding the Linux file system hierarchy and managing storage resources are critical tasks for system administrators. You will learn how to create and manage partitions, format filesystems, mount and unmount devices, and maintain disk space efficiently.

210 3. Package Management

Linux distributions utilize package management systems to handle software installation and updates. Familiarity with package management tools, such as **apt** or **yum**, will empower you to install, update, and remove software packages seamlessly.

211 4. System Updates and Upgrades

Regularly applying system updates and upgrades is essential for ensuring the latest security patches and feature improvements are in place. You will learn how to manage system updates effectively and handle major version upgrades.

212 5. Network Configuration

Configuring network interfaces, setting up DNS, and managing routing are crucial tasks in Linux. Understanding tools like **ifconfig, ip**, and **route** will help you configure network settings effectively.

213 6. Process Management

Monitoring and managing processes is essential for optimizing system performance and troubleshooting issues. You will learn how to use tools like **ps, top**, and **htop** to view running processes and manage their priorities.

214 7. Backup and Recovery

Data loss can be catastrophic, and having a reliable backup and recovery strategy is a must. You will learn different backup methods and how to restore data when needed.

215 System Administration Best Practices

216 1. Create a Standardized Environment

Establishing a standardized environment with consistent configurations and software packages simplifies system administration and reduces potential conflicts.

217 2. Regularly Backup Data

Perform regular backups of critical data to ensure you can recover in the event of system failures, data corruption, or cyberattacks.

218 3. Practice Safe Remote Access

Enforce secure remote access policies, such as using SSH for remote connections and implementing VPNs for secure network access.

219 4. Implement Monitoring and Alerts

Set up monitoring tools to track system performance and generate alerts for potential issues, enabling proactive responses.

220 5. Test Changes in a Safe Environment

Before making significant changes to the production environment, test them in a sandbox or development environment to avoid unintended consequences.

221 Advanced System Administration Techniques

222 1. Kernel Management

Understanding the Linux kernel and how to manage kernel modules, compile custom kernels, and tune kernel parameters can optimize system performance.

223 2. Performance Tuning

Profiling system performance and fine-tuning resource allocation can significantly enhance the Linux environment's responsiveness and efficiency.

224 3. Security Hardening

Implement security hardening measures, such as disabling unnecessary services, configuring firewalls, and utilizing SELinux or AppArmor to enhance system security.

225 4. Virtualization and Containers

Exploring virtualization technologies like KVM and containerization platforms like Docker and Kubernetes can lead to more scalable and resource-efficient solutions.

226 Conclusion: Mastering System Administration Essentials

Congratulations! You have delved into the realm of System Administration Essentials and equipped yourself with the skills to take charge of your Linux environment. System administration is a continuous learning process, and as you gain experience and encounter diverse scenarios, your proficiency as a Linux administrator will grow.

Remember, effective system administration is not only about solving immediate issues but also proactively managing and optimizing the Linux environment to ensure it runs smoothly and securely. By adhering to best practices, leveraging automation, and staying informed about advancements in Linux technologies, you will be well-prepared to tackle any challenge that comes your way.

In the next chapter, we will explore the world of Linux Networking, where you will learn about network configurations, services, and security measures. So, keep on learning, keep on experimenting, and enjoy your journey as a skilled Linux system administrator!

CHAPTER 8

ADVANCED LINUX TOPICS

Elevating Your Expertise

Welcome to Chapter 8 of our comprehensive guide, where we embark on an exciting journey to explore Advanced Linux Topics. In this chapter, we will elevate your expertise by delving into more complex and sophisticated aspects of Linux, catering to both experienced users and those seeking to expand their knowledge. From mastering the intricacies of the Linux shell to understanding server configurations, we will equip you with the skills to take your Linux proficiency to new heights.

227 Mastering the Linux Shell

228 Understanding the Shell

The Linux shell is a command-line interface that allows users to interact with the operating system directly. As an advanced Linux user, becoming a master of the shell is essential for efficient and powerful system administration and development tasks.

229 Shell Scripting

Shell scripting enables you to automate repetitive tasks and execute complex commands with ease. You will learn about variables, conditionals, loops, and functions, empowering you to write sophisticated scripts for various purposes.

230 Advanced Command Usage

Exploring lesser-known command-line options and advanced utilities will enhance your efficiency. Topics such as **awk**, **sed**, and **grep** offer powerful text processing capabilities, while **find** and **xargs** help you manage files and directories more effectively.

231 Linux System Internals

232 Understanding the Linux Kernel

The Linux kernel is the heart of the operating system, responsible for managing hardware resources and providing essential services. We will dive into the inner workings of the kernel, including process scheduling, memory management, and device drivers.

233 Working with Kernel Modules

Kernel modules allow you to extend the kernel's functionality without recompiling the entire kernel. You will explore how to load, unload, and configure kernel modules to enhance your Linux environment.

234 Systemd and Service Management

Systemd is the modern init system used in most Linux distributions. Understanding systemd unit files and service management is crucial for effective system administration, including managing services, timers, and targets.

235 Advanced Networking and Security

236 Network File Systems

Network File Systems (NFS) enable file sharing across networks. We will cover NFS configuration, security considerations, and mounting remote directories on client machines.

237 Virtual Private Networks (VPNs)

Building upon the networking concepts introduced earlier, you will explore VPN technology in more depth. Learn to set up and configure VPN servers and clients, enabling secure and encrypted communication between remote systems.

238 Network Security: Firewalls and Intrusion Detection

Enhancing network security becomes increasingly important as your Linux environment grows. You will learn about setting up firewalls, using tools like **iptables** and **ufw**, and implementing intrusion detection mechanisms to protect your systems from potential threats.

239 Server Configurations and Optimization

240 Web Servers: Apache and Nginx

Web servers are critical components for hosting websites and web applications. We will delve into Apache and Nginx configurations, virtual hosts, and performance optimization techniques to ensure optimal server performance.

241 Database Management: MySQL and PostgreSQL

Databases are essential for storing and managing data. You will explore MySQL and PostgreSQL, learning about database administration, backups, and replication to maintain robust and reliable database systems.

242 High Availability and Load Balancing

For mission-critical services, high availability and load balancing are paramount. Discover techniques like clustering, failover mechanisms, and load balancers to ensure uninterrupted service availability.

243 Conclusion: Elevating Your Linux Expertise

Congratulations on reaching the end of Chapter 8, where we explored Advanced Linux Topics and elevated your expertise to new heights. By mastering the intricacies of the Linux shell, diving into system internals, and exploring advanced networking and security concepts, you have grown into a seasoned Linux user capable of handling complex tasks with confidence.

As you continue on your Linux journey, remember that learning is a never-ending process. Stay curious and keep exploring new technologies, tools, and best practices. Advanced Linux topics are continuously evolving, and staying up-to-date with the latest advancements will empower you to stay ahead in the ever-changing world of Linux.

In the final chapter of our guide, we will wrap up this comprehensive journey with a glimpse into Future Trends in Linux and provide guidance on furthering your expertise. So, embrace your newfound knowledge, continue to experiment, and revel in the endless possibilities that Linux has to offer!

CHAPTER 9

LINUX IN THE CLOUD

Navigating the Future of Computing

Welcome to Chapter 9 of our comprehensive guide, where we embark on an exciting exploration of "Linux in the Cloud." As technology continues to evolve, cloud computing has emerged as a game-changing paradigm in the world of computing. Linux, with its flexibility, scalability, and open-source nature, has played a central role in shaping the cloud computing landscape. In this chapter, we will dive into the evolving relationship between Linux and cloud computing, providing insights into this transformative integration and the endless possibilities it offers for the future of computing.

244 Understanding Cloud Computing

245 The Rise of Cloud Computing

Cloud computing has revolutionized how businesses and individuals store, process, and access data and applications. It offers on-demand access to a pool of computing resources, including storage, processing power, and networking, over the internet.

246 Cloud Service Models

There are three primary cloud service models:

1. **Infrastructure as a Service (IaaS)**: Provides virtualized computing resources, such as virtual machines and storage, over the internet. Users can deploy and manage their own software on these virtualized resources.

2. **Platform as a Service (PaaS)**: Offers a development platform with pre-configured environments and tools, allowing developers to focus on building and deploying applications without managing the underlying infrastructure.

3. **Software as a Service (SaaS)**: Delivers fully functional applications over the internet, eliminating the need for users to install, maintain, or manage the software locally.

247 Linux's Integral Role in the Cloud

248 Open-Source Nature

Linux's open-source nature aligns perfectly with the philosophy of cloud computing, promoting collaboration and innovation among developers and users worldwide. As the most widely used operating system in cloud environments, Linux has become the foundation for countless cloud-based solutions.

249 Compatibility and Customizability

Linux's compatibility with various hardware architectures and its customizable nature make it an ideal choice for building cloud infrastructures tailored to specific needs. Its versatility allows for seamless integration with cloud services, enabling businesses to design cloud solutions that suit their requirements.

250 Resource Efficiency

Linux's efficiency in resource utilization is a significant advantage in cloud environments, where optimizing resources is critical. Its lightweight footprint ensures that cloud instances consume minimal resources while delivering high performance.

251 Cloud Deployment Models

252 Public Cloud

Public clouds are operated and managed by cloud service providers, offering computing resources to the public over the internet. Linux-based virtual machines are a staple in public cloud environments, providing scalable and cost-effective solutions for a wide range of applications.

253 Private Cloud

Private clouds are dedicated infrastructures that serve a single organization. Linux's flexibility and customizability enable businesses to build private cloud solutions that align perfectly with their specific security, compliance, and performance requirements.

254 Hybrid Cloud

Hybrid clouds combine both public and private cloud deployments, allowing organizations to leverage the benefits of both models. Linux's compatibility with various cloud platforms facilitates seamless integration and workload portability across hybrid cloud environments.

255 Linux in Cloud Services

256 Containerization with Docker

Docker, a popular containerization platform, leverages Linux containers to package applications and their dependencies into lightweight, portable units. This enables easy deployment and management of applications across different cloud environments, promoting scalability and consistency.

257 Kubernetes: The Orchestration Master

Kubernetes, an open-source container orchestration platform, is another groundbreaking development driven by Linux. Kubernetes streamlines the management of containerized applications, automates scaling and resource allocation, and enhances high availability in cloud environments.

258 Linux and Serverless Computing

Serverless computing abstracts the underlying infrastructure, enabling developers to focus solely on writing code without worrying about server management. Linux plays a crucial role in serverless computing, powering the runtime environments that execute serverless functions.

259 Cloud Security and Linux

260 Securing Linux Instances

Ensuring the security of Linux instances in the cloud is paramount. Best practices for securing Linux in cloud environments include regular updates, employing strong authentication methods, and implementing strict access controls.

261 Data Protection and Compliance

Linux provides robust data protection capabilities, which are essential in cloud environments where data may traverse different networks. Encrypting data in transit and at rest, as well as adhering to compliance regulations, safeguard sensitive information in the cloud.

262 Network Security and Firewalls

Implementing network security measures, such as firewalls and intrusion detection systems, is crucial in cloud computing. Linux's powerful tools like **iptables** and **fail2ban** aid in safeguarding cloud instances from potential threats.

263 The Future of Linux in Cloud Computing

264 Cloud Native Technologies

As cloud-native technologies continue to evolve, Linux will remain at the core of their development. The convergence of Linux, containers, and Kubernetes will redefine how applications are built, deployed, and managed in the cloud.

265 Edge Computing

Edge computing, which brings computation and data storage closer to the location of data sources, is an emerging trend. Linux's lightweight and adaptable nature makes it an excellent fit for edge devices and gateways, enabling efficient data processing and real-time analytics at the edge of the network.

266 AI and Machine Learning

Linux's prominence in cloud computing will further extend to artificial intelligence and machine learning. Cloud-based machine learning platforms, powered by Linux, will enable organizations to harness the potential of AI for data analysis, pattern recognition, and decision-making.

Navigating the Future of Computing with Linux in the Cloud

In this chapter, we embarked on a journey to explore the fusion of Linux and cloud computing, witnessing how Linux's adaptability, resource efficiency, and open-source philosophy have made it the driving force behind the cloud revolution. As cloud computing continues to shape the future of computing, Linux will remain a cornerstone in this transformative landscape.

As you navigate the ever-evolving world of Linux in the cloud, seize the opportunities it offers to innovate, collaborate, and develop cutting-edge solutions. Embrace the endless possibilities, stay curious, and keep exploring the horizons of Linux in cloud computing, as it becomes the backbone of the next generation of computing technologies. The possibilities are limitless, and the future is bright, so let's embrace the future of computing, powered by Linux in the cloud!

CONCLUSION

Congratulations! You've reached the end of this comprehensive journey through the fascinating world of Linux. We've covered everything from the fundamentals of Linux to advanced topics, exploring its integration with cloud computing and peering into the future of this remarkable operating system.

Throughout this book, we've equipped you with the skills and knowledge to become a proficient Linux user, whether you're a beginner or a seasoned professional looking to expand your expertise. From mastering the Linux shell, understanding system administration essentials, and exploring networking and security, to elevating your skills with advanced topics and diving into the world of cloud computing, you've gained a well-rounded understanding of Linux and its immense potential.

Linux's open-source nature and versatility have made it the backbone of countless technologies, driving innovation in various industries. As you continue on your Linux journey, don't forget to embrace the collaborative spirit of the open-source community. Share your knowledge, contribute to projects, and engage with fellow Linux enthusiasts to foster growth and progress.

Remember, learning Linux is an ongoing process. Stay curious and keep exploring the latest advancements and trends in this er-evolving field. Leverage the power of Linux to build robust, scalable, and secure solutions, whether you're managing a personal system, developing applications, or deploying enterprise-grade services in the cloud.

As we navigate the future of computing, with Linux as a guiding force in the cloud, the possibilities are boundless. Embrace the endless opportunities, seek out new challenges, and continue to expand your expertise. Whether you're building cutting-edge applications, securing critical systems, or leading the way in emerging technologies like AI and edge computing, Linux will be there, empowering you every step of the way.

Thank you for joining us on this Linux adventure. We hope this book has not only equipped you with practical skills but also ignited your passion for the world of open-source computing. As you forge ahead, remember that the Linux community is vast and supportive, offering a wealth of resources and fellow enthusiasts to connect with.

May your Linux journey be filled with discovery, innovation, and the joy of exploring this incredible operating system. Embrace the challenges, celebrate the victories, and continue to push the boundaries of what's possible with Linux by your side.

Happy exploring, and may your Linux endeavors lead you to new horizons!

With warm regards, Ryan

www.ingramcontent.com/pod-product-compliance
Lightning Source LLC
LaVergne TN
LVHW051246050326
832903LV00028B/2591